The No-Nonsense Guide to Dividend Growth Investing

Jesse R. Blair

Copyright © 2021 by Jesse R. Blair

All rights reserved.

Foreword

It was January 2009.

The stock market had crashed from the record highs of September. Every day brought more despair and more losses to the market. There appeared to be no end in sight. I, like many, was feeling crushed and despair watching my investment accounts evaporate daily. All this, just when I thought I was getting ahead.

Having suffered thru the tech crash of 1999, the Great Financial Crisis was nearly enough to make me want to give up investing altogether.

I remember sitting in my comfy recliner, holding my old Mac book, and looking through my investment account. I was trying to decide which stocks I might as well sell to claim tax losses when I noticed something strange in the transaction history.

There plain as day was a deposit made in the name of one of my stock positions that was nearly as large as the value of the stock itself. OK, so it wasn't quite that large. In my state of despair, it seemed much bigger. However, it wasn't insignificant, and

I quickly scanned the transactions for other such deposits.

Sure enough, there was at least one more significant deposit. These were, of course, dividend payments. I was aware of dividends before this, of course. However, they were always an afterthought. Dividends were that tiny amount of money stocks paid you for owning them. The real reason for investing was to increase my portfolio value. How wrong I was…

Fast forward to today.

My entire investing philosophy has changed. No longer do I worry about the day-to-day fluctuations in the market. My portfolio balance is just a vanity number. Instead, there is only one number that I focus on now:

The number that leads to financial freedom.

Today I focus only on the income my portfolio generates. Dividend growth companies provide an ever-growing income stream. These are companies that continually pay increasing dividends. Instead of worrying about a stock market downturn, I welcome them! My portfolio doesn't require much work or attention as I buy stocks with the intent to hold them forever.

Having been thru the dot-com bubble (2000-2002) and the Great Recession (2007-2009), I needed a new investing style. Focusing on income growth is a total change in philosophy and low stress compared to worrying about the overall portfolio balance. I wish I could say I didn't make any mistakes along the way, but I would be lying. I made plenty!

Table of Contents

Foreword iii

Introduction 1

Welcome to Dividend Growth Investing 3

High Dividend vs. Dividend Growth Investing 7

What is dividend growth investing? 12

Dividend Achievers: Kings, Champions, Aristocrats, and more! 15

Selecting Dividend Growth Stocks 19

Stock evaluation 32

Additional Useful Metrics 63

The importance of Leadership 75

Portfolio Design & Considerations 80

Bucket Based Approach to DGI Portfolio Design 89

When to Sell 112

ETFs in Dividend Growth Investing 126

Odds and Ends 132

Common Mistakes and Pitfalls 147

Definitions 152

Questions or Comments? 156

Free DGI resources 156

Introduction

This book is for you whether you are new to investing or an investing veteran considering dividend growth investing. Some terms within the book may be unfamiliar to the novice investor. At the beginning of each chapter, a quick glossary provides simple definitions for that chapter. These terms will be in bold. At the end of the book is a complete set of definitions.

Dividend growth investing isn't complicated, and a book about it shouldn't be either!

This book isn't about showing a bunch of numbers to convince you that dividend investing is a better strategy than anything else. If you are reading this, you are open to the idea of dividend growth investing. Instead, this book is about sharing the basics of DGI (dividend growth investing) to see if the strategy resonates with you and your goals.

Dividend growth investing is not a get rich quick plan. It is an entirely different type of philosophy than most types of investing.

Dividend growth investing is rather dull. The companies that make up the dividend-growth universe are generally boring. There is no trading to do. There's no getting excited when the market is up and worrying when it's down. Mostly, it's about waiting. It's waiting for the price to be right to buy; Waiting for the next dividend check to come. And it's watching the income grow over time.

"Investing should be more like watching paint dry or watching grass grow. If you want excitement, take $800 and go to Las Vegas." – Paul Samuelson

Welcome to Dividend Growth Investing

dividend yield – The dividend yield is a ratio of the amount of money a company pays shareholders for owning a share of stock divided by its current stock price. This is expressed as a percentage and usually on an annual basis.

cost basis – The cost basis is the original purchase price of a stock.

A dividend is a distribution of part of a company's earnings to its shareholders. Profits are usually the source of dividends. Most of the time, US stocks pay dividends quarterly, although some pay annually, bi-annually, or even monthly. Many companies pay no dividends at all.

There are many reasons a company might not pay a dividend. Some companies don't make a profit, so there is no money to distribute to shareholders. Other companies are fast-growing and need to reinvest all the profits back into the business. Some investors see paying a dividend as a sign that the company has no growth prospects. They view this as a sign of weakness in the company. At the same time, other investors see a company's ability to generate enough cash to send some to stockholders as a sign of strength.

There is also an argument of tax inefficiency around dividends. When a company makes a profit, the company pays taxes. Then, when the company makes a dividend distribution to stockholders, the stockholders pay taxes on the dividend received. Many investors argue this double taxation is a reason not to be in favor of companies paying dividends.

Investors that argue against dividends focus on capital gains. Capital gains are when a stock goes up in price, and then you sell it. Dividend growth investing is, in essence, the opposite of this method of investing. It doesn't matter if the stock goes up, down, or sideways with dividend growth investing.

Dividend growth investors focus on dividend income. Watching the income grow is the goal, not the value of the portfolio. However, it requires a company to continue to grow earnings to increase dividends continually. A natural result of increasing profits is an increase in the stock price over time.

There are several reasons why some investors prefer companies that pay dividends.

Dividend-paying stocks create income – Probably the most common reason individuals will invest in dividend-paying stocks is for the income they provide. Many investors like the fact that their investment will generate income without having to sell the stock.

Dividend-paying stocks tend to be more stable – Generally, companies that can pay dividends are well established, with consistent profits. Many companies transition to paying dividends as they grow and mature.

Many investors see dividends as a hedge against the stock price falling – This works in two ways. Firstly, a dividend tends to support a stock price. As a stock price falls, its **dividend yield** will go up. The dividend yield is the annual amount paid divided by the stock price. Eventually, the yield reaches a point where more investors buy the stock, supporting the price. Secondly, many investors view collected dividends as lowering their **cost basis** in a company. While this isn't true from a tax standpoint, it can be from a psychological perspective.

It works like this:

You own a share of stock XYZ. You paid $100 for your share. You collected $10 in dividends over the past two years. Currently, the stock is trading at $90 per share. While the stock's value may now be $90, you are still even with the $10 in dividends collected. Additionally, you still own the position, which you expect to continue to pay more dividends in the future.

Some stocks a **DGI** investor has held for a long enough time may collect more per year in dividends than the price the investor paid to buy the company in the first place!

"The stock market is a device for transferring money from the impatient to the patient." – Warren Buffett

High Dividend vs. Dividend Growth Investing

dividend cut – A dividend cut is a reduction in the dividend from the previous payout. For dividend growth investors this is usually measured on an annual basis.

economic cycle – The economic cycle is the fluctuation of the economy between periods of growth and contraction.

MLP – A master limited partnership (MLP) is a business venture that exists as a publicly traded limited partnership. For this reason, it has some of the tax benefits of a partnership but is easy to trade like a public stock.

REIT – A real estate investment trust (REIT) is a company that owns, operates, or finances income producing properties. A special class of REITs called mREITs focus on mortgages.

It is easy to confuse High-Dividend investing with Dividend Growth Investing. Both strategies are seeking to achieve an income stream thru dividends. However, this is where the similarities end.

The risks of high dividends are well advertised. This is for a good reason. Generally, high yields are a sign that investors believe a business is in trouble. In these situations, investors consider the stock "high risk" for a **dividend cut**. In this case, high risk means that there is a high probability that the company will reduce the dividend in the future. Dividend growth investing, by its very definition, seeks to avoid dividend cuts.

However, in High-Dividend Investing, investors seek out very high dividend-paying stocks. This form of investing is perfectly fine for some individuals. It tends to require much more work than Dividend Growth Investing because the dividend quality tends to be lower.

Dividend quality refers to how safe the dividend is. Higher quality dividends are less likely to be cut or reduced. For this reason, a High-Dividend investor will need to research and monitor stocks constantly as they seek to avoid dividend cuts and reposition money as reductions occur.

Additionally, investors focusing on high yields will also consider preferred stocks and high yield bonds. In contrast, a DGI investor will generally pass on these as they do not tend to grow dividends over time.

So why include information on High-Dividend Investing at all? Well, for two reasons: 1.) Many people confuse the two, so it is crucial to understand the difference, and 2.) Some stocks overlap in both types of investing, and it's important to understand this aspect.

Occasionally, some stocks will both have high yields and continue to grow the dividend. This overlap can occur for several reasons. Some industries traditionally have higher than average yields. Even the slightest negative market sentiment will drive the yields up higher still. This condition sometimes makes them attractive to both High-Dividend Investors for the current yield and Dividend Growth Investors because they continue to grow the dividend. These industries historically include communications, tobacco, and energy (oil and gas).

As investors anticipate changes in the **economic cycle**, they move money from one industry to the next. Industries that are popular today will likely not be the same ones popular ten years from now. As this happens, high-quality companies will have prices (and yields) that go up and down.

This cycling is not always indicative that a stock is failing or a superstar. Remember, DGI investors are looking over a period of many economic cycles.

There is a resource section near the end of this book. Some of these resources have historical dividend information on stocks. Taking the time to research the highest yield a company has offered during its history is a fantastic insight into the possibilities. The stock market is cyclical, and the chances are that if a company has offered a higher yield in the past, it will happen again in the future.

Additionally, some DGI investors choose to include high dividend stocks in their portfolios as part of a larger strategy. Usually, in this situation, investors will keep the positions small and understand they are taking a risk. Using high dividends stocks will be discussed further in the portfolio design chapter.

Throughout this book, sometimes the term dividend is used and sometimes distribution. While for most practical purposes they are the same to a DGI investor, they are not identical.

The most significant difference comes at tax time. Each has different tax consequences. The vast majority of companies will have "qualified" dividends. These use the capital gains tax rates. There are certain types of companies like **MLP**'s and **REIT**'s that have capital gains distributions. Income tax rates apply to these distributions. For most DGI investors, the difference is minor compared to the overall goal of building a steady income stream. Consider speaking with an accountant to understand the full tax implications.

Note: *MLP's use a K1 form at tax time. These are issued late and can be confusing. MLP's do offer some tax advantages in a taxable account. However, MLP's can create issues in a tax-deferred account, like an IRA. Although this is uncommon without a very large position. If you have concerns over the taxation or the use of K1, please discuss with an accountant.*

"I think you have to learn that there's a company behind every stock and there's only one real reason why stocks go up. Companies go from doing poorly to doing well or small companies grow to large companies." – *Peter Lynch*

What is dividend growth investing?

dividend growth stock – A dividend growth stock is a company that steadily increases dividends over time.

initial yield – The initial yield is the dividend yield an investor expects to receive at the time a stock is purchased.

So, what is Dividend Growth Investing? Simply put, Dividend Growth Investing is focusing on growing a stream of dividend income over time. Dividend growth investors believe a portfolio that provides a steady and growing stream of dividend income is the best way to finance a secure retirement. This income comes without having to worry about the fluctuation of stock prices.

A dividend stream of income is real money. You can reinvest it in more dividend growth stocks or other uses like day to day living expenses.

A dividend growth investor isn't concerned with capital appreciation because we never know when the stock market will go up (or down).

Instead, a dividend growth investor is concerned with the dividend's safety and its growth potential.

Most investors ask, "What's my account's current value?" A dividend growth investor asks, "How much dividend income did my portfolio generate?"

Most investors ask, "How much was my account up or down this year?" A dividend growth investor asks, "How much did my account's income grow this year?"

Most investors ask, "Where is the stock market going this year?" Dividend growth investors don't try to predict short-term swings in the market. In fact, DGI investors welcome market downturns. Market dips are the best time to go bargain shopping for more **dividend growth stocks**. During pullbacks, **initial yields** are higher on high-quality companies.

Generally, dividend growth investors focus on high-quality companies with high-quality earnings. Many of these companies are in mature industries. They are boring. You generally won't find these companies in the headlines for how much the stock has gone up (or down). Instead, most of these companies have had steady profits over decades.

There is a group of dividend growth stocks that have been growing the dividends for over 50 years!

These are called the Dividend Kings.

"Wall Street makes its money on activity; you make your money on inactivity." – Warren Buffett

Dividend Achievers: Kings, Champions, Aristocrats, and more!

portfolio – A portfolio is a collection of stocks.

There are a few select groups of stocks on which a dividend growth investor will generally focus. These include the Dividend Kings, Aristocrats, Champions, Contenders, and Challengers. These are lists of stocks that have raised dividends annually for a set number of years. Generally, these will only include US stocks because of the difficulties in adjusting for foreign currency fluctuations.

Thru the link at the end of the book, resources are available that link to the lists.

The first of these is the Dividend Kings, which have been growing the dividends every year for over 50 years. That means these companies have been thru many economic downturns, crises, and political climates and still have managed to continue growing the dividend.

Consider that Dividend Kings have raised dividends thru all the following:

At least seven recessions, including the Great Financial Crisis of 2008-2009 and the Dot-com bubble of the late '90s

The 1970's oil crisis and stagflation of the 1970s

The Vietnam war, the collapse of the Soviet Union in 1991, 9/11, and both Iraq conflicts

High interest rates of the 1980s

The COVID-19 pandemic of 2020

It is no wonder that DGI investors covet these stocks!

It is true that occasionally a company on the Dividend Kings list does fail to raise the dividend and will fall off the list. However, it is far more likely that companies on this list will continue to grow the dividend, as they have a proven track record. As of this writing, there are around 30 companies that fit the Dividend King criteria.

Dividend Aristocrats is a list maintained by Standard and Poors (S&P). This is a group of stocks included in the S&P 500 that have raised dividends for 25 years. They must also meet specific size and liquidity requirements.

Then finally, we come to the Champions, Contenders, and Challenger lists. Dividend Champions are stocks that have raised the dividend for 25 years. Contenders and Challengers are stocks that have been growing for at least 10 and 5 years, respectively.

Private individuals maintain these lists. Unlike the Aristocrats list, these don't have size requirements and include all known stocks meeting the criteria. Generally, these are all US-based stocks due to the difficulties of measuring dividend growth as foreign currency exchange rates fluctuate.

These lists contain over 700 individual stocks! These lists represent every industry. Additionally, every size company can be found, from the extremely large mega-cap to the tiny micro caps. You can find similar lists for Canadian, UK, and European stocks that are measured in their local currencies.

As we move into selecting stocks for a Dividend Growth **portfolio**, these lists represent the research's starting point. Keep in mind that all investments come with risk. The goal of selecting individual stocks is to minimize risk. Specifically, as a DGI investor, the risk we want to consider is, "will this company continue to pay and raise the dividend well into the future?"

In general, a company that has increased dividends for 50 plus years is considered a safer dividend than one that has been paying for five years. They are "battle-tested," as shown above. It is worth considering all the stocks as potential candidates and weighing the risks accordingly.

For the sake of simplicity in this book, these lists collectively will be referred to as dividend achievers. Keep in mind that there is an actual group of dividend achievers that includes dividend Champions (25+ years), Contenders (10+), and Challengers (5+). The official dividend achiever list is maintained separately from the Kings and Aristocrats.

> *"An important key to investing is to remember that stocks are not lottery tickets." – Peter Lynch*

Selecting Dividend Growth Stocks

dividend growth rate – The dividend growth rate is the annualized rate, expressed as a percentage, that a dividend has grown over a set amount of time. Usually this is expressed as a 1-year, 5-year, or 10-year growth rate.

dividend safety – Dividend safety refers to how likely is a dividend likely to be cut or reduced. A safe dividend is unlikely to be cut.

Investing is all about reducing risk. Selecting individual stocks is a part of this. All stocks have risks. A dividend growth investor has different risks to consider than other types of investors. Most types of investors are primarily concerned with the stock price going up. While price appreciation is nice, a DGI investor's primary concern is to create a steady and *GROWING* stream of dividend income.

Here are the primary concerns for determining if a company can and will continue to pay and raise dividends into the future.

Will the company continue to grow profits into the future?

Does the company generate enough cash flow to continue to pay and raise dividends?

Is the company in an industry that will continue to flourish (or exist) for the next 20, 30, or even 50 years?

Does the company have a history of raising the dividend?

Does management have a strong case for growing the company and making it thrive?

Everyone always wants to know, "What yield should I look for?" and "What dividend growth should I target?". These are complex questions, and the real answer is "it depends." We will discuss this in detail. First, it is important to cover the basics of choosing a solid stock that satisfactorily answers the above questions.

Dividend Growth Investing is a long-term strategy. Having quality companies in your portfolio is more critical in the long run than having any particular "yield" in mind.

Below are common factors that DGI investors consider when evaluating a stock. Some investors will choose to use additional metrics not covered here. There are any number of metrics available. However, it is generally true that there is diminishing returns on making an evaluation more complex.

There is a saying that direction is more important than speed. This saying can be especially true for DGI investors as the investments are long term.

DGI investors want a broad picture over the next several decades. They are not trying to predict stock performance over the next year or even five years.

There are three things a DGI investor wants in an investment: A good initial yield, a strong **dividend growth rate**, and to buy at a good value. Finding all three is rare. When an investor can get two out of the three, they should snatch up the stock!

Pre-selecting stocks for further evaluation:

Most investors use a set of criteria before beginning a full evaluation of a company. The most common pre-screens for a DGI investor are years of dividend growth, dividend growth percent, and current dividend yield. These are all relatively easy to determine.

The "years of dividend growth" metric is where our dividend achievers come into play. Typically, the longer a company has been increasing the dividend, the more likely it is to continue growing into the future. This expectation is from a business standpoint and a policy standpoint. The business end is the fact these companies have been thru many economic conditions and still raised dividends. The policy end is the company's commitment to growing the dividend. Companies with a short dividend growth history may suddenly reverse course on raising or even maintaining payouts.

There is a tradeoff here.

Companies that have been raising dividends for 50 years generally tend to grow dividends at a more modest pace, while companies with a shorter history tend to grow faster. This relationship is not a hard-fast rule but a generality.

An investor should require a set years of growth to invest in a company. Companies with at least 25 years of increases will be the safest selections. However, many companies with less than 25 years of growth are worth considering, as well.

For example, many tech companies have only recently begun paying dividends. However, they have massive potential for dividend growth. Many of these companies generate large profits and have minimal capital expenses. (Although they can be research and development intensive.)

An investor must always consider risk. Companies with fewer years of payout growth will almost always carry more risk.

Dividend growth rates

The dividend growth rate is the annualized percentage of growth in a stock dividend over a set time. Usually, dividend growth is expressed as a 1-year, 5-year, or 10-year growth rate.

Dividend growth can be calculated by hand using a company's dividend per share and an online compound annual growth calculator. Dividends per share are easy to find online, but you can use the company's financials to calculate them. The calculator will require three pieces of information, the starting dividend per share, the ending dividend, and the number of years included. Many investors prefer to use a website to get dividend growth rates rather than calculating the growth rate themselves.

Using a financial website is a much quicker method and meets the requirements of most investors. Most websites will provide a fixed period of dividend growth, such as the 5-year or 10-year dividend growth rate. An investor who wants to find the growth rate outside the website's window will need to calculate it by hand.

The goal of the DGI investor is to have a steadily growing income stream. This requires dividend growth. Any company a DGI investor invests in should have dividend growth unless it fills a particular need in the portfolio (see portfolio construction).

So, what should an investor seek when it comes to dividend growth?

To answer that question, we need to first explore dividend growth rates in general. Consider nearly any Dividend King. This company will have grown its dividend every year for over 50 years! Would you expect its dividend to have grown at the same rate every one of these years? Of course not!

Over the last 50 years, all the Dividend King companies have seen many economic cycles and events. Additionally, most of these companies will have faced innovation challenges forcing them to reinvent themselves. Most of these companies will have experienced periods of slow growth and times of fast growth. The dividend growth rates will reflect this, as well.

Just because a company is quickly growing the dividend today doesn't mean it will always rapidly expand into the future. Conversely, a company that is barely growing the dividend today might not always grow it so slowly going forward. A DGI investor should evaluate each company on its own merits and future prospects.

Every investor would love a company with a very high dividend growth rate. A very high growth rate could be considered anything over 20%. The thing to remember about very fast dividend growth: *It's not going to last forever.*

There are a couple of things to consider when evaluating a company with a very high dividend growth rate.

The first is how sustainable is this dividend growth? Sometimes a company will grow the dividend by increasing the amount of profits paid out as dividends (see payout ratio in the next chapter). Growing this way works for a while, but eventually, there is no more room to grow the dividend. Additionally, paying out too much of the profits creates a risk to the **dividend safety**. The distribution may need to be reduced (cut) or eliminated in an economic downturn.

The second thing to consider with a company that has a very high dividend growth rate is its starting dividend yield. A company that is growing its dividend quickly by increasing profits is fantastic. However, these companies tend to command higher valuations, and most of the time, have meager dividend yields. In fact, the dividend yields are often low enough that most DGI investors find them not worth it. But these stocks make excellent candidates to put in a watchlist to purchase if they fall enough during a stock market drop.

Most stocks in the dividend growth universe will have 5-year growth rates between 2 and 20 percent. Dividend Kings and Champions will generally trend toward the lower side as they are usually in mature industries.

A good rule of thumb to know is the "rule of 72." This rule is an easy way to estimate a future value, not just of dividends but anything with a growth rate. It works like this: Divide 72 by the growth rate, and the resulting answer is the number of years to double.

A company with a dividend growth rate of 8% would take nine years to double the dividend. That is, 72 / 8 = 9. Notice that you express the growth rate of 8% as a whole number, not 0.08.

Every investor should consider their goals in looking at dividend growth rates to target. Most investors will consider anything under 5% too low. While anything over 15% needs to be considered unlikely to be maintained for many years. There is nothing wrong with companies with dividend growth rates over 15%. However, for forecasting the future, a rate that high may be unrealistic.

Current Dividend Yield

The current dividend yield is the most common place investors begin their search for stocks.

The current yield is a great place to start because it is immediate income and is a known variable. However, it is easy to fall into the trap of focusing too much on initial yield. After all, a 5% yield on a $1000 investment is $50 per year, while the same investment on a stock yielding 1% is only $10.

Additionally, the current yield is a fixed number. Dividend growth streaks have no guarantee of continuing. At the same time, dividend growth rates are a backward-looking metric. A current yield is guaranteed, at least so far as the company continues paying a dividend. With all the variables involved with investing, it's nice to have a known constant.

Unfortunately, concentrating on current yield is a very short-sighted approach. It will almost always lead to future dividend cuts or low dividend growth. Dividend cuts are one of the worst things that can happen to a DGI investor trying to grow an income stream. Additionally, slow dividend growth leads to sub-optimal performance over time.

The best place to start is always to consider the dividend increase streak. Starting with the increase streak is made easy using the Dividend Achiever lists. Selecting a stock from these lists is the quickest and easiest way to reduce dividend cuts. Screening the lists for an acceptable yield and growth rate will further narrow the selection.

Putting it all together

Most DGI investors would love to purchase stocks with a current yield of 3% and a dividend growth rate of 10%. This is an excellent mix of both current yield and dividend growth. However, there are no hard rules, and each investor should determine what best meets their needs. Typical ranges for targeting current yield might range from 2.5% - 4%, and dividend growth might be 5 – 12%. But most investors will make exceptions at one time or another.

Current yield and dividend growth rates tend to be inverses of each other. It is unlikely for a stock with a high dividend yield to have a high dividend growth rate. Although, it is not uncommon to find stocks with relatively low dividend yields that also have relatively low dividend growth. Often, these stocks are ones with very long dividend growth streaks. People are willing to pay for dividend safety.

Very few DGI investors will invest in a stock yielding less than 1%, even if the dividend growth rate is exceptionally high. Usually, these are growth stocks. For many DGI investors, the risk of the company maintaining a high dividend growth rate far enough into the future to offset a low starting dividend is just too much.

An investor who chooses individual stocks by merely sticking with dividend growth streak, dividend growth rate, and current dividend yield will most likely do great with dividend growth investing. It's easy to find complex analysis of dividend growth stocks online using all kinds of metrics. Some of these metrics can be useful but think of them as icing on the cake. The three metrics above will comprise 80% of the results.

Authors note:

I target a minimum current yield of 3% and require a 5-year dividend growth rate of at least 7%. This is because I want my income stream to grow at a rate of 7% annually without investing new capital or reinvesting the dividends. Using the rule of 72, this equates to doubling my income approximately every ten years.

I determined the 3% minimum yield because I am currently reinvesting dividends into more stock. The 3% starting yield on new stocks plus the 7% growth equates to a 10% overall income growth in my portfolio. Growing at 10% allows my income stream to double approximately every seven years. (72/10).

These starting points don't mean that I only buy stocks with a 3% or better dividend. I have purchased stocks with starting dividend yields as low as 2% if I am very confident in the company's ability to grow the dividend at 7% or better well into the future. I do, however, offset these purchases with higher starting yield stocks. In this way, I maintain an overall starting yield of 3% on new investments.

"Value stocks are about as exciting as watching grass grow, but have you ever noticed just how much your grass grows in a week?" – Christopher Browne

Stock evaluation

payout ratio – The dividend payout ratio is the amount of dividends paid to investors as a percentage of earnings. Sometimes this is expressed as a percentage of cash flow.

Once potential investment candidates have been determined using dividend streak, dividend growth rate, and initial yield, the list can be further refined using some reasonably simple metrics. The pre-selection process has eliminated most of the risk by selecting candidates with long dividend growth streaks. Additionally, we have picked stocks that meet our income and growth goals by using our desired starting yield and dividend growth.

The next step in stock selection is to reduce risk further. The metrics discussed here are, for the most part, only useful to DGI investors. These metrics will help identify possible reasons why the dividend might not be sustainable and avoid "overpaying" for a stock. Purchasing at a good value is another way to describe not overpaying.

In DGI investing, "overpaying" is very investor specific. DGI investors are looking at very long time frames, usually 20 years or longer. Some investors go so far as to plan on never selling. So, the argument becomes that it doesn't matter what price you pay if the company can continue increasing its dividend, and it meets your pre-selection requirements.

There is a truth that over a very long time frame, that initial price shouldn't matter. However, many DGI investors are also "value" investors. Value investors want to buy stocks at bargain prices. This method makes sense because the better the bargain, the higher the initial starting yield.

In this situation, the investor sees the starting yield similar to starting a new job. They want to negotiate the highest salary possible because each annual raise will compound on top of the previous.

While either philosophy is fine and works quite successfully in DGI investing, the choice is highly personalized. Perhaps the best and most straightforward answer is to try and not overpay for a company. The concept of overpaying is much more tied to "Growth" investing. Growth investors focus on growing the overall value of the portfolio.

While DGI investors concentrate on increasing the income stream, most would also like to see the value of their portfolio grow as well.

Refining the Selection Process

Although many investors like to make it so, selecting stocks for a DGI portfolio should not be complicated. A few simple metrics will yield similar results to more complicated and time-consuming methods. Many analysts and paid services need to make it seem complicated to justify what they provide.

First, we begin by creating a list of potential stocks by screening the dividend achievers. The screen uses the desired years of growth, initial yield, and growth rate. Next, we perform a simple analysis. Below are the basic metrics that most investors need to select individual stocks for a DGI portfolio. Using the dividend achievers lists as a starting point removes most of the risk. In this instance, risk refers to selecting a poor DGI company.

Payout Ratio

The first and arguably most important metric for a DGI investor is the **payout ratio**. The payout ratio is arguably the best way to determine the safety of a dividend. Additionally, it is relatively easy to calculate or find online.

Simply defined, the payout ratio is the percentage of earnings paid out as dividends. Sometimes, instead of earnings, cash flow is used in the calculation. Each method has pros and cons. We will discuss each in some detail, as this metric is a critical concept in considering a dividend-paying company.

The formula for this calculation looks like this: DPR = total dividends / net income.

Where DPR = Dividend payout ratio.

The dividend payout ratio shows the percentage of a company's earnings paid out as dividends to the shareholders. This metric tells us a lot about the health of a company's dividend. A very low payout ratio indicates the company is using most of its earnings to reinvest in the company.

Companies that are growing the business faster tend to have smaller payout ratios. These companies use the earnings to reinvest in the company to continue growing. Additionally, a company with a low payout ratio can indicate that a dividend is safe, and the company has room to continue to grow the dividend in future years.

Conversely, a high payout ratio can indicate that a dividend might be at risk of being cut or eliminated. A company with a payout ratio greater than 100% indicates that the company pays out more dividends than it earns in income. Many investors view this as a sign the company's dividend is at high risk. However, just as saying a high dividend yield is risky, the same goes for payout ratios. Although, a payout ratio over 100% almost always indicates significant risk.

When evaluating dividend payout ratios, the industry that a company operates in matters. For example, industries such as utilities and telecoms have very stable earnings over the long term. Additionally, these companies tend to be mature and slow-growing. They usually have "safe" dividends even though they will have higher payout ratios than companies in other sectors.

Many companies operate in cyclical industries. A cyclical industry is one that sometimes booms and sometimes busts. They generally move with the business cycle and make significantly more money during economic prosperity and less during downturns. Examples of cyclical industries are heavy equipment manufacturers, restaurants, clothing, and airlines. Anything that people tend to buy more of in good times and less in bad times will be considered cyclical. It Is important to recognize if a company is cyclical when considering payout ratios.

Cyclical companies generally need to have lower payout ratios during good times. This lower payout ratio is to ensure that they can continue the dividend during slow times. A cyclical company with a high payout ratio during an economic boom will be at a much higher risk if the economy weakens. When the economy slows, their earnings will be expected to fall, possibly leaving them with an unsustainable dividend.

Essentially, there is no correct number for a dividend payout ratio. Many DGI investors use a cutoff of 60% when evaluating companies. Using 60% is a reasonable number and generally considered "safe." One significant advantage of using a simple payout ratio like this is the numbers are readily available. On nearly any stock quote, the EPS, earnings per share, and dividend amount are available. This data makes the payout ratio readily available by a simple calculation of DPS (dividend per share) / EPS (earnings per share).

There is one caveat to using a simple payout ratio based on earnings and dividends paid. Most sources report earnings using generally accepted accounting principles (GAAP). GAAP earnings can create large swings in earnings that have no impact on a company's ability to pay a dividend.

These swings occur because GAAP earnings include everything, including one-time charges. Items that do not happen on a repeating basis are one-time charges. One-time charges can be both positive or negative for earnings.

Items that positively affect earnings might be the sale of a division. In contrast, negative items include writing down an acquisition or restructuring costs. While these costs affect earnings, they don't reveal anything about a company's ability to continue paying a dividend. Think of it like this:

You own a house that you can make the monthly mortgage on comfortably. You decide to get an appraisal on the house. The assessment will affect your net worth. But, will the outcome of the appraisal affect your ability to pay the mortgage? Of course not! Your ability to make money is the driver in paying the mortgage, not the value of your house.

While this is not a perfect analogy, it demonstrates how one-time charges on a company's earnings don't affect its ability to pay a dividend. However, a company that continually makes poor business decisions leading to write-downs and one-time charges may have other problems.

Because of the nuances when using GAAP earnings when calculating the payout ratio, many DGI investors prefer to use other methods. One of the easiest to use is adjusted earnings, sometimes referred to as operating earnings. Another popular but more difficult to find metric is using a company's cash flow in the calculation.

Adjusted earnings back out one-time charges from the GAAP earnings. These more accurately reflect what the business would have made in ordinary circumstances. Using adjusted earnings helps smooth the payout ratio when looking at it over multiple years.

Another way of looking at payout ratios is by using the cash flow from a company's operations.

Ultimately, cash generated by the company pays the dividend distribution. For this reason, many DGI investors prefer using this method. In some situations, a company can generate earnings, but not cash.

The calculation for this is relatively straight forward:

Total dividends paid / Cash from operations

It is essential to use cash from operations in this calculation and not the total cash flows. The total will include cash from investing and from financing. The purpose of looking at the payout ratio is to help determine if a company can continue to pay its dividend from its business operations.

Using a simple payout ratio with either adjusted earnings or cash from operations will suffice for most companies. However, some industries can require different payout ratio calculations. These tend to be very capital intensive, like pipelines or utilities. Additionally, real estate investment trusts (REITs) have their own set of accounting rules.

Pipelines will provide a number called the distributable cash flow. When calculating the payout ratio for a pipeline, use the distributable cash flow. It gives a clear picture of the company's ability to continue to pay dividends. However, this is not an easy number to calculate.

The distributable cash flow is nearly always provided in the company's financial statement. Unfortunately, most financial websites will not have this number readily available. So, it can take some research to look at historical figures to find trends.

A real estate investment trust, or REIT, is a company that owns, operates, or finances income-generating real estate. REIT's have a different set of accounting rules than traditional companies. They use a term called funds from operations, or FFO.

A payout calculation on a REIT then becomes:

$$\text{Total distribution} / \text{FFO}$$

However, REITs generally issue more shares to fund capital projects. Real estate is a very capital-intensive business. When looking at the trend of FFO, it is essential to look at it on a per-share basis. Looking at it on a per-share basis ensures that the new shares issued are supporting the distribution.

How to use the payout ratio

There is no perfect way to use the payout ratio in determining if a company is a good selection. Here are some general guidelines. These are discussed in detail further below:

A low payout ratio is good. Most DGI investors like to see a payout ratio under 60%, although in some industries and in some situations, 80% is acceptable.

The payout ratio history is just as important as at any point in time. Ideally, you want to see a modest change in the payout ratio over time.

In general, a low payout ratio is a good sign. A low payout ratio indicates that a company has room to grow its dividend and is unlikely to be cut in an economic slowdown. Of course, a low payout ratio is relative to other companies in the same industry.

Some industries, like tech, can require constant innovation to stay competitive. Generally, in sectors like this, the lower the payout ratio, the better. The low payout ratio usually indicates the company is investing in research and development or saving for future acquisitions.

Other industries have higher payout ratios in general. These can be utilities, which have a steady income, often guaranteed. Others can be in established non-cyclical sectors that don't require a lot of capital projects. Many consumer staples companies will fall into this category.

It is worth considering the overall size of a company as well. Size applies to both overall payout ratio and looking at the trend over time. A company making $10 million per year in profit may not sustain paying out 50%, as this would leave it with only $5 million to reinvest. In contrast, a company generating $10 billion per year in profit might be able to pay out more than 50%. A company this large may have trouble finding places to invest $5 billion back into the company.

The payout ratio history can give us insight into the health of dividends in a few ways. The first is when we are evaluating cyclical stocks. Cyclical stocks tend to make more profit in a booming economy and less in a slow economy. Cyclical stocks include heavy equipment manufacturers, clothing, travel, and banks, among others. Looking at the payout ratio trend over time, we can better understand what the ratio is doing. During the boom part of a cycle, payout ratios might appear very low, and then during the downturn, they will appear very high.

The other thing we look for when we look at the history of payout ratios is the overall trend. Has the ratio increased with time or stayed flat? A company that has increased its dividend by increasing the payout ratio may not sustain increases at the same rate in the future.

It is not uncommon to see payout ratios increase significantly as companies transition from high growth to slower growth. This change occurs because a young company will need to use its earnings to help pay for development. When growth slows, the company can now pay out more dividends. The company needs to invest fewer profits back into itself.

The goal of a DGI investor is to grow the income stream. Growing income means selecting stocks that consistently grow the dividend. One of the criteria many investors use is the dividend growth rate, expressed as a 1-year, 5-year, or 10-year average. A stock with an especially high dividend growth rate may be very appealing to an investor. A high growth rate indicates that the dividend is growing rapidly. Payout ratio trends become very important when looking at very high dividend growth rates.

A company that has been growing the dividend quickly by merely increasing the payout ratio, paying out more of the earnings as dividends may not sustain this growth in the future. This factor is especially true if the ratio approaches 60-80%. That range is the upper-end target that most investors consider safe.

Dividend yield vs. Historical dividend yield

The payout ratio is an excellent way to evaluate the safety of a dividend. However, it does little to tell us about the value of a stock. While there are numerous ways to value a stock, one of the best ways for a DGI investor is to use the historical dividend yield.

The historical dividend yield is comparing its current yield to its historical average yields. Some investors compare over a set time range, while others look at all available data. The biggest drawback to using a shorter timeframe is recency bias. Stocks sectors tend to come in and out of favor over time. Industries in favor will have lower yields. At the same time, industries out of favor will have higher yields.

In the late 2010s, technology stocks were in strong favor. Being in favor pushed the yields below 1% for many companies. These same stocks were out of favor in the early 2010s. During this time, many yields were closer to 3%. Using only recent history is a mistake. It can fool an investor into thinking a stock is a bargain when it's not. The theory of using historical dividend yield assumes that dividend yield will revert to the average over a long enough time.

Besides just looking at the historical average, it is useful to look at the dividend yields during recessions. These time frames give insight into what is likely to happen during the next downturn.

During the Great Recession of 2008-2009, many stocks with a historical average dividend yield of under 3% hit double digits. In March 2020, at the start of the Covid pandemic, many companies matched the Great Recession yields.

Consider the following:

A stock with an average yield of about 3% falls in price during a recession and now yields 6%.

This particular company has been growing the dividend at a rate of 8% consistently.

By the rule of 72, it takes nine years for this dividend to double (72/8). After nine years, an investor buying at the average yield will have a yield-on-cost of 6%. (Yield-on-cost is the current dividend divided by the initial price paid for a stock.)

Compare this to an investor who purchased during the recession. The yield of 6% will essentially create a nine-year head start!

This example is why every DGI investor should be interested in buying stocks at bargain prices. In this case, bargain prices mean a yield that is above the average for that company. Unfortunately, buying at a good discount isn't always easy.

Buying in a recession when the stock market is falling fast is scary for most investors. Seasoned DGI investors focus on the dividend stream. But even they don't enjoy watching the value of their portfolio drop sharply. During these times, it is doubly important to focus on the income stream produced by the portfolio. At the same time, investors should recognize the potential of adding more companies. Especially stocks that typically have initial yields too low for consideration.

Waiting for economic downturns can take a long time. On average, a recession occurs once every five years. However, in more recent history, the periods are getting stretched longer and longer. Maybe it will revert to the mean at some point but waiting a decade is a long time. Many dividend growth stocks will have doubled the dividend or more in a decade.

Finally, buying at a big discount is generally contrarian investing. During a recession, nearly every stock will be way down in price. Outside of a recession, stocks tend to be at bargain prices for a reason. Sometimes an entire sector is out of favor. Other times a company may have real financial problems.

Due diligence should flush out financial issues. Due diligence is the evaluation portion of stock research. However, the talking heads on TV and blog posts on the internet will constantly be trashing bargain stocks. This constant slamming is the real challenge.

Negative opinions can cause a DGI investor to second guess. It is essential to keep in mind the time frames involved. All of the television personalities and most of the articles focus on the short term. Talking about where a company will be in 20 years does not make these people money. Where a company will be in 20 years does make DGI investors financially free!

A DGI investor needs to learn to tune out all the noise from these sources. Focus instead on the metrics and long-term outlook. Dividend Kings and Champions have survived many situations. The odds are they will continue to do so. True, over time, some will end up cutting dividends or even failing as a company. The vast majority will continue to pay and increase dividends well into the future.

Additionally, a DGI investor should find sources of information that align with dividend growth values. These will never be on TV. Television is an instant gratification media device. Instead, look for articles that have a focus on dividend growth investing. Read several different sources and learn which sources and authors resonate with your investing philosophy. Finally, be wary of sources that claim to be DGI oriented yet slant towards high dividend investing. These can lead you away from the "growth" portion of DGI investing.

Everyone enjoys buying at a discount. Who doesn't like to brag to their friends about the great deal they got? But what is more important than a great deal is not to overpay. Just as in our example of buying at a great yield gives a head start to the income stream, overpaying is a major roadblock.

Understanding the concept of not overpaying is the real power of using historical dividend yields. A yield will revert to the mean much more often than a recession will come along. The stock market sees a correction, or a 10% drop, on average every 8 to 12 months. So, the chances are that many companies an investor is interested in will reach or exceed the historical average yield every year at some point.

Historical PE ratios

A PE ratio is a simple ratio for valuing a company. It measures the current share price versus the earnings per share. By taking the current share price divided by the earnings per share, we get the PE ratio. However, we rarely need to calculate it by hand. Nearly every stock quote will include the PE ratio.

Some DGI investors prefer to work with historical PE ratios to determine if a stock is at a good buy point. Historical ratios offer a simple way to compare valuations at different points in time. This method is not significantly different than using historical dividend yields. Usually, when a stock is trading at a price that creates a higher than average dividend yield, it will have a lower than average PE ratio.

One of the advantages of using the historical PE ratio is that it is slightly simpler. Finding the exact historical average PE ratio or the last five or 10-year average can be challenging. However, many investors will use a simple rule. Often they will use a "rule of thumb" average of 15. So, if a PE is below 15, they consider it a likely bargain. When the PE is higher, they deem it overpriced.

While using a "rule of thumb" is quick and easy, it can lead to mistakes. Some faster-growing dividend growth stocks may have an average PE of 20 or more. Many of these will be of extremely high quality or have meager dividend yields.

Generally, using this rule of thumb is mostly used to see if a stock is severely overvalued. For most companies that a DGI investor considers, a PE of 15 is reasonable. However, it's critical to recognize that a PE of 17 or 13 won't necessarily mean that a stock is over/underpriced. Mostly it will mean that it's about average. Again, not overpaying is the biggest concern over a long time frame, so this quick and dirty method works just fine in most cases. Starting with stocks from the dividend achiever's universe reduces the risk of getting it wrong.

There can be many nuances with PE ratios. Ratios can use trailing or forward earnings, GAAP earnings, or adjusted earnings. A full description of all of these is out of the scope of this book. But, a DGI investor should be aware they exist.

For DGI investors, using a trailing PE with adjusted earnings is most appropriate. This is for the same reason adjusted earnings are best to work with when considering payout ratios.

Note: Often, with PE ratios, the letters TTM appear. These letters stand for "trailing twelve months."

This term means the PE ratio uses the earnings over the past 12 months in the calculation.

What's the story?

There are a lot of stocks in the world from which to choose. Fortunately for a DGI investor, the process doesn't need to be complicated.

About 6000 stocks are trading on the US exchanges (NYSE and Nasdaq). Of these, roughly 2400 pay dividends. When we consider stocks that have increased dividends for at least five consecutive years, we now only have 750 companies. The list narrows to 400 companies when we look at ten years of dividend growth.

Using the Dividend Kings/Champions/Contenders, etc., is where every DGI investor should begin.

Starting with dividend achievers narrows the number of potential stocks considerably. Having a predetermined minimum starting yield and dividend growth requirement will further refine the list. An investor should research the stocks surviving this cut for both risk and value.

Researching for risk and value does not need to be a complicated process. Many analysts will go into great depth and use all sorts of metrics to determine if a stock is a good buy. The fact is that for a DGI investor focusing on the long term, that looking at payout ratio and either a historical dividend payout or PE ratio will be just as accurate.

Remember that DGI investors are focused on the very long term. No analyst (or any person) can predict the long term with any accuracy. Even companies themselves do a poor job of estimating earnings more than a few quarters out.

If a DGI investor were to take the evaluation process discussed thus far and never do another bit of research or reading, they would be just fine most of the time. There is a very subjective factor in stock selection for a DGI investor as well. This factor is simple, "Will the company be around in 20 or more years and still increasing the dividend?"

Nobody knows the answer to this question. Starting with our lists of dividend achievers, we know that there is a high likelihood that the dividends will continue to grow in any given year. Yet, every year there is a small percentage of companies that fall off the lists. This possibility is why each investor needs to consider the "story" behind a company. What are the reasons it can succeed? Why might it fail?

The most common reason DGI companies fail is from a failure to innovate, which includes being replaced by new technology and more nimble competitors. There are times where new laws and regulations have the potential to hurt a DGI company as well.

Even considering the possibilities of disruptive technology isn't overly useful. For at least the past 20 years, renewables will replace oil and coal. 3-D printing is going to revolutionize production and put industrials out of business. The examples go on and on. At the time of this writing, electric cars will replace internal combustion, and digital payment systems will eliminate cash.

Over time, new and innovative technologies always overtake the old. Assuming they provide a better solution for the end consumer. The part is knowing the timing. New technologies tend to creep into our world and are seen as a minor issue to the existing status quo, until seemingly overnight they are the status quo.

An example of this is the evolution of music. For years, music stores kept CDs in a tiny section. Nobody knew much about CDs. Then seemingly overnight one day, cassettes were gone, and only CD's remained. Then perhaps one day a friend was showing you a new MP3 player. MP3 players were a bit of a novelty at first. Then one day suddenly, everyone had one. And now, very few people purchase digital songs when they can subscribe to a service and make playlists.

At every stage of this innovation evolution, the new technology started with a small following, and it grew slowly, until BAM! It reached a tipping point. Nearly overnight, the latest technology became the standard. There are many examples of this occurring. At one time, digital cameras were a novelty. Does anyone even own a digital camera anymore?

The point is every company existing today is susceptible to being replaced. It is up to the individual investor to determine if they believe in a company's ability to innovate and change. While at the same time recognizing that disruptions don't occur overnight. A DGI investor doesn't need to follow the day to day changes in the stock market.

They need to follow the story of a company or industry and pay attention to the evaluation metrics.

Following a company's story is difficult because it plays out over a long time. Consider any company. On any given day, some pundit will declare the company doomed on TV or in an article. Bad press happens regularly for most companies.

Any number of incidents create bad press. These include products getting recalled, drugs failing in trials, or even an employee making bad choices that end up on social media. Sometimes a rival company's great new product is the threat. Other times, it's new laws that will end the company. The number of reasons the company will fail is limited only by imagination. Most of this is just noise.

It is impossible to know if a company's story is to succeed in the future or be replaced by something new. The most important thing to remember is that if stock selection begins with proven dividend growers, these companies have overcome plenty of adversity. In any given year, they will most likely grow the dividend again. Regardless of what you read, these companies are proven winners.

The second thing to consider is the foundation on which you purchased a company. Because DGI investors try to buy stocks at a bargain, there is a built-in cushion. If the payout ratio was low, the company could make changes or weather a downturn.

Finally, it's worth remembering that companies don't disappear overnight. Usually, there are warnings. No investor is perfect. Everybody has a company that fails them once in a while. Paying attention to a company's payout ratio can help ease sustainability concerns. And watching dividend growth rates can provide insight into how a company views its future growth prospects. However, some other metrics can also be useful to the DGI investor.

Authors note:

In the past, I've used some rather complicated methods of selecting stocks for my DGI portfolio. But I have found that I get the best results for considerably less work by sticking to the dividend achievers lists and applying simple tests using the payout ratios and historical dividend yields.

I like to see payout ratios of less than 60%, but this is not a hard-fast rule for me. I look at the industry and compare other companies in the same industry. Additionally, I covet companies with payouts under 35%. I see these as having the potential to grow the dividend well into the future.

The biggest caveat to using payout ratios, in my mind, is to make sure you look at the historical trend.

I want to know if the payout ratio fluctuates wildly, is it steady, or is it increasing rapidly or slowly. None of these by themselves mean anything without further digging into a company.

Historical dividend yields are my favorite metric. My personal goal is to purchase a stock paying out in the top 25% of starting dividend yields that it has historically seen. However, I am happy buying a company at its average historical yield if it has a low dividend payout ratio, and I really like the company's "story."

While I prefer using historical dividend yields, historical PE ratios are usually just as useful and sometimes easier to find.

I like historical numbers because stocks tend to revert to the mean over a long enough time frame. At least, this reversion is easy to see with stocks followed by DGI investors. Young growth stocks do not have a long enough history to make this case. However, it can be frustrating as stocks can trade at levels well above or below the historical average for years. But, there exists one real challenge with historical numbers.

Historical numbers can be hard to find. Therefore, many investors will prefer to use a rule of thumb with PE ratios. Some resources exist that can help an investor with historical numbers. Unfortunately, most of the best resources are subscription-based. The resource list in the back has many of these.

Anymore, I focus more on a company's story than I used to. I trust stocks on one of the achiever lists. While I never use a company's story to justify overpaying, I have used it to avoid or even reduce positions.

In recent years, I have begun reducing and eliminating positions in oil-producing companies. I still hold natural gas pipelines and refiners. I could be missing out on some great bargains; however, I am finding the future 20 years out for oil companies somewhat murky. I do not doubt that some of these oil-producing companies will survive in some form. Very likely, some will still be increasing dividends. I feel like there are better places to put my money and help me sleep at night.

Another common story at the time of this writing is the potential changes to our (the US) healthcare system. This potential has pushed down the price of insurers and drug manufacturers into the bargain zone. I am avoiding the health insurance companies as I don't have a firm understanding of how a future healthcare system might affect them. On the other hand, I am buying drug companies as I believe no matter what changes, they will still be needed and allowed to profit in some form.

Notice that these are all very personal decisions to me. Only the future will tell if my choices have good results or missed out on great deals. I would rather miss out on a great deal than suffer a future dividend cut. The best I can do is follow the stories and re-evaluate as the future unfolds.

I recommend reading articles with a skeptical view as most try to get eyeballs and not necessarily help a long-term investor. But I find them useful in understanding the arguments for and against a particular stock. These arguments assist in evaluating the story. Looking at multiple viewpoints can offer a check before falling in love/hate with a specific industry or company.

> *"Learn everyday, but especially from the experiences of others. It's cheaper!"* – John Bogle

Additional Useful Metrics

earnings per share (EPS) – The EPS is a financial calculation that divides the total earnings of a company divided by the total number of shares. This results in the earnings attributed to each individual share.

Dilution – Stock dilution is when a company issues more shares thereby reducing the percentage of the company owned by prior shareholders. This in turn reduces the EPS of the company as the earnings are now divided by more shares.

Buyback – When a company performs a buyback, it is buying back shares of its own company. This is the opposite of dilution and increases the EPS as fewer shares exist.

Everything discussed up till now could be considered essential. This chapter will discuss a few additional metrics that can be useful but certainly not needed to make good DGI stock selections. There are, of course, any number of metrics an investor might choose to examine. Many metrics are just twists and combinations of others.

Keeping it simple tends to lead to the best results without overthinking.

Credit Rating

Nearly all companies use debt in some form. Even companies that generate vast amounts of cash. The reasons vary, and debt is not necessarily a bad thing. A corporate credit rating is an assessment of the likelihood that the company will default on its debt.

Three agencies assign credit ratings. These are Moody's, Standard & Poor's (S&P), and Fitch Ratings. The ratings they provide help investors determine the level of risk involved with investing in a company.

The ratings each agency provides are a spectrum of various possibilities. The ratings range from the highest quality to default. Unfortunately, each rating agency has unique designations for the quality of debt. It can take some time to learn the designations, but fortunately, you can easily find these online.

ADDITIONAL USEFUL METRICS

Table 1: Credit Agency Bond Ratings

Moody's	Standard & Poor's	Fitch	Grade	Risk
Aaa	AAA	AAA	Investment	Lowest Risk
Aa	AA	AA	Investment	Low Risk
A	A	A	Investment	Low Risk
Baa	BBB	BBB	Investment	Medium Risk
Ba/B	BB/B	BB/B	Junk	High Risk
Caa/Ca	CCC/CC/C	CCC/CC/C	Junk	Highest Risk
C	D	D	Junk	In Default

The single most important thing for the DGI investor is to avoid any company with a "junk" rating. Obviously, the higher the company's rating, the less likely it will default on its debt. A higher rating also means the dividend is likely safer as well.

The highest possible rating is AAA or Aaa, depending on the agency. As of 2020, only two companies have the highest credit rating, Johnson & Johnson and Microsoft. Both companies are Dividend Achievers. Johnson & Johnson has increased the dividend for 58 consecutive years. At the same time, Microsoft has increased its dividend for 19 straight years. In fact, as of 2020, both these companies have a higher rating than the US government!

Checking a company's credit rating is a good idea before investing to make sure it is investment grade. It will be pretty rare to find a company with a long dividend growth history (15+ years) with a "junk" credit rating, but it is not impossible.

While not common, it's also important to know that some companies won't have a credit rating. Not having a rating can be for a variety of reasons. Any companies on a Dividend Achiever list and that don't have a rating are because they choose not to and don't need one. A company must pay to be assigned a rating. It may not be worth it for a smaller company that doesn't take on a lot of debt.

Earnings Per Share Growth (Past and Projected)

To continue to grow a dividend over time, a company will also need to grow its earnings. Of course, a company could also increase its payout ratio to increase the dividend.

Watching the payout ratio is an excellent way to assess how the company is growing the dividend. However, earnings growth is a metric that can be used hand in hand with the payout ratio. Additionally, earnings growth can offer a glimpse into the future.

Analysts are always running projections on the prospects of companies. Companies themselves usually offer guidance for the next year and adjust every quarter as results come in. Some analysts will even project 5-year or 10-year earnings. Sometimes this is called a growth forecast. Whatever you call it, it is a flawed exercise.

Consider these a guide.

There are too many unknowns to know the future with any degree of certainty. The further into the future the projections, the less likely they are to be accurate. Earnings projections might offer a useful insight into direction, but not magnitude. If anyone were capable of predicting the future, they would be doing something else.

It is safe to say that a company with 5-year growth projections of 20% has brighter prospects than a company with forecasts of 5%. But, except for random chance, it is doubtful either of these will be exact.

Instead, look at the past **earnings per share** (EPS) growth. We use earnings per share for two primary reasons. The first is to level out any **dilution** from issuing new shares. Issuing new shares is unusual for DGI stocks (except REITS). The second is because many companies do stock buybacks. **Buybacks** are buying their own shares. When a company buys its shares, it causes the earnings per share to increase. Earnings per share is total earnings divided by the total number of shares. So, by buying back shares, the total number of shares is reduced. Additionally, earnings per share is an easy to find metric.

There is a saying that past performance does not guarantee future results. This is true. Understanding the past helps us understand a company's story allowing us to evaluate future prospects.

There are several things to consider when looking at the past EPS. What is the average growth rate over the period? Is the growth rate accelerating, slowing, or is it flat? Are there any large changes from one year to the next? Is the growth lumpy, does it have up and down years, but is it generally trending up?

All of these work together to help form the story. As an investor weighs these considerations, it is important to be asking, "Why?" Determining the reasons all of these occurred is understanding a company's past. When we know the past story, it's possible to ask if the story fits going forward.

Ideally, we will see a positive growth rate, hopefully matching or beating the dividend growth rate. Earnings growth exceeding the dividend growth rate isn't critical. But slower earning growth may lead to lower future dividend growth. It's essential to try and understand how a company has grown over time.

Past growth becomes part of the story.

How the growth rate is changing gives clues as to the future of a company. A slowing growth rate may be because consumers are switching to a competitor's product, or simply that the company has grown so big that the rule of large numbers is causing it to slow. Try to determine why the growth rate is changing. Is it a mature industry? Did they launch a new product? Buy another company? Sell part of the company? Another reason? Is the company in a cyclical industry? All of these become part of the story of the company.

The past story lays the groundwork for predicting the future. Look at the past and ask, "What's changed?" How likely will the factors that built the past continue? What would have to happen to change this story? This practice is different than trying to estimate future earnings. This approach is much more holistic. Once an investor builds a story, they should continuously review it to make sure it still makes sense as the future unfolds.

> *"Know what you own and know why you own it." – Peter Lynch*

Authors note:

I don't dwell over any of these metrics. I generally make sure that the companies I invest in have an investment-grade rating. Even with this, I generally don't bother looking it up unless I want to add a company with a very high rating.

Anymore, I am aware of the stories of most companies in the Dividend Achiever's lists. Therefore, I don't spend a lot of time looking at earnings growth when considering a stock. I will usually look up the past five or ten-year growth rate and compare it to the dividend growth rate. This review is to make sure everything is reasonable. If I see something alarming, such as the dividend growth rate far exceeding the EPS growth rate, I will research why. Then when I understand why, I will examine if it changes my story for the company.

I do tend to look at the future earnings projections. I like to compare them to the past and look for large changes. Both of these numbers are relatively easy to find, and it is not a time-consuming activity. When I see a big difference between the past and predicted future, I spend time to understand why. I evaluate the reasons and make my conclusions. Then I examine my existing story for a company and decide if I need to change it.

Storytelling is by no means an exact science. Predicting the future never is. For that reason, I tend to think of my story as a string of probabilities, knowing full well that anything I believe about a company's future could prove to be wrong.

I read a lot of articles about companies. I don't read to find opportunities to invest. After all, most media exists to get clicks, not to help investors. I read them to see what stories are out there and to learn what I might be missing in my own.

A great example of deciding on a company's story was Microsoft in the early 2010s. The media was pushing a particular story. However, the media is only focused on the short term and getting clicks.

From 2012 to 2015, the company experienced what was virtually no growth. As a result, the stock price, already depressed from the 2008 recession, was not keeping up with the broader market. The story was that people hated the newest windows products.

Microsoft lacked the cool factor, and competitors like Apple would eat their lunch going forward. Essentially Microsoft was considered dead money.

However, the counter-story, largely ignored by the media, was much more optimistic. Windows was still the dominant operating system with no replacement in sight. Its video gaming division, Xbox, was growing, as was its cloud storage. Although at the time, gaming and cloud storage was a small chunk of the business. Additionally, the sheer magnitude of the cash generated by the company was enormous.

At this time, Microsoft was yielding close to 3%. The business was growing the dividend at 20% per year and had a payout ratio of around 30%.

The massive challenge for a DGI investor is sorting thru stories and numbers. Then the investor must decide what story to believe and investing accordingly. Often it means investing in stocks that are out of favor. In this particular case, I chose to invest primarily because the Windows operating system was the dominant system. In the worst case, I figured the company would grow the payout ratio for a while to increase the dividend. Additionally, I knew acquisitions weren't out of the question with a huge cash pile, which could spark future growth.

The story I created for Microsoft didn't play out quite like the one I made. But, I had also developed a downside story that I felt was low risk. In reality, Microsoft started growing its earnings again, to the tune of nearly 20% per year.

Whenever a stock is doing poorly, the media will spin stories of doom and gloom for the company. I like to ask myself if the reasons are likely to apply 20 years from now. Is the company working to move in a new direction? What bright spots exist within the company, and what are their prospects? Cash is king. A company with a large cash pile and generating lots of money can use it. (Granted, many make poor purchases.)

One of the key considerations I like to take when constructing a story is management. I often give companies with a history of good leadership the benefit of the doubt.

Not that this is an easy thing to determine. Like much of constructing a story, there is no hard metric for this and is often a gut feeling from media, comments, and knowledge.

> *"In the short run, the market is a voting machine. But in the long run, it is a weighing machine." – Ben Graham*

The importance of Leadership

Companies with poor leadership tend to flounder, no matter how much of an advantage the business seems to have over competitors. Conversely, great leadership will allow a company to survive and thrive even in the most dire of situations.

Evaluating management is a very subjective process. No metric can indicate good leadership. Often analysts will hail an increasing stock price as a sign of successful management. However, a company focused on managing the stock price is probably not focused on long-term success. Every DGI investor should be concerned with the future.

Looking at a company's culture is very useful in determining the quality of a management team. Culture is beneficial when focused on the long term. Is the business known for treating employees well? Are they always working to come up with new products and innovations? Conversely, do they downplay competitor innovations that might be a threat?

Before 2007, Apple's most significant source of revenue was the iPod. Apple came out with the iPhone in 2007, knowing it could replace its greatest source of income. Not many companies have leadership willing to sacrifice revenue. Apple was looking to the future.

Consider Kodak.

Kodak invented the digital camera in the 1970s. They buried the technology because management couldn't see how this fit their business. Their primary revenue source was film. How could something that doesn't use film possibly be good for the company? Kodak was not a forward-looking company.

It's easy to look at these examples in hindsight. It's much more difficult to recognize them as they are happening. Listening to a company's leaders speak about the future and its competitors is a good place to start. Just remember they will never say anything overtly negative about their own business. Conversely, when a company downplays a rival, consider if they are short-sighted.

One of the more useful creations in recent years for considering the culture is sites like Glassdoor,

Indeed, and other job boards. On these sites' employees can leave reviews of a company. Just remember that reviews tend to slant towards the negative as unhappy people tend to leave comments.

Sometimes a CEO is hated for one reason or another. An unpopular CEO is often apparent in articles. But mostly, it becomes evident in the comments. There can be a lot of confusion around this, as often, investors blame stock performance on the CEO.

A CEO who focuses on stock performance is most likely not acting in the best interest of a company's future. Be especially leery of a CEO with a finance background. For example, a CFO made CEO in a technology company hardly sounds like a visionary leader.

Stock performance by itself is a weak indicator of leadership. Any number of factors affect stock performance. A significant variable is market sentiment. Sometimes the entire sector is performing poorly. More telling is a company that is underperforming all its peers. In these instances, the investor should examine the management and culture closely. You can tell a lot about management's quality by judging what they've accomplished compared to the competition.

Look at an organization's past. Have they made good acquisitions? Did the purchases add to the company or detract? Most merger's that promise cost savings and "synergies" end up costing investors. Companies that successfully integrate acquisitions usually have strong leadership.

Interestingly, investors often proclaim mergers as great for a business, but spinoffs tend to release more shareholder value.

Judging management is not an exact science. Very little of investing is. The great investor Warren Buffet believes the quality of management is a critical factor in making sound investments. Here is what he has to say on judging leadership:

"I think you judge management by two yardsticks. One is how well they run the business, and I think you can learn a lot about that by reading about both what they've accomplished and what their competitors have accomplished, and seeing how they have allocated capital over time."

"Look at what they have accomplished, considering what the hand was that they were dealt when they

took over compared to what is going on in the industry."

"You want to figure out ... how well that they treat their owners. Read the proxy statements, see what they think of — see how they treat themselves versus how they treat the shareholders. ... The poor managers also turn out to be the ones that really don't think that much about the shareholders, too. The two often go hand in hand."

Portfolio Design & Considerations

Market capitalization – Commonly referred to as market cap, the market capitalization of a company is its total number of shares times the current share price. Companies are commonly referred to as large-cap, small-cap, mid-cap, and micro-cap.

large cap – A large cap stock is a company with market capitalization above $10B.

small cap – A small cap stock is a company with a market capitalization of between $300M and $2B.

Everything covered thus far has been about selecting individual stocks. Now, we will consider how to build an entire DGI portfolio. A DGI investor should craft a portfolio to do two things; meet the investor's goals and minimize risk.

Firstly, an investor should decide on the goals of the portfolio. Many factors might affect an individual's goal. For a DGI investor, at some point, the investor will want to stop re-investing dividends and use the income to pay bills. Additionally, some investors may desire a higher overall yield and others more dividend growth. Others may be most concerned with the safety of the income stream.

The one thing a DGI investor should not be overly concerned with is the portfolio's market value. Instead, the focus should be on a growing stream of income. Investors concerned with maximizing the overall market value have a different approach to portfolio construction. DGI investors win when stocks go up, AND they win when stocks go down.

Humans tend to perceive negative events much more strongly than positive ones. Even the most staunch DGI investors feel it when the stock market is down 40%. However, a DGI investor will understand that the portfolio's goal is to grow an income stream. A DGI investor can watch the portfolio's value drop while the income stream continues to grow.

The real power of dividend growth investing is experiencing a large market drop and watching the income continue to grow. At that point, a DGI investor truly understands the power of dividend growth investing.

Stocks go up, stocks go down, but the income continues to grow. An experienced DGI investor waits patiently for a stock market correction to buy top companies at bargain prices and historically high starting yields.

Diversification

Diversification can mean a lot of things. Generally, when people talk about diversification in a portfolio, they mean diversifying across sectors or industries. However, it can also mean **large-cap** vs. **small-cap**, international stock vs. US-based, growth vs. value, the number of positions owned, or any number of factors. The point of diversifying is to reduce risk. For most investors, this means lowering the downside risk during a correction.

A DGI investor's goal is to protect the income stream. The goal is not to prevent a drop in total portfolio value. Although, due to the nature of DGI stocks, a DGI portfolio will tend to drop less in a market correction.

The measure of a dividend-growth portfolio is the income it produces. Not necessarily total income, but quality, sustainable income is the goal. The portfolio's total market value should never be the measuring stick.

There are two primary considerations a DGI investor in reducing risk to the income stream. The first is sector risk, or the chance that an entire sector cuts dividends. The second is individual stock concentration risk, or having a large percentage of income from a single stock.

Diversifying across sectors

Having too much invested in one sector adds risk to the portfolio. A downturn in the sector could cause many companies to freeze or cut dividends. This situation occurred at the end of 2015 when oil prices collapsed, causing many oil companies to cut their distributions. Energy companies were hit again during the Covid-19 pandemic, as were many REIT's (Real Estate Investment Trusts).

Concentration in a sector usually occurs on accident, not by design. Industries can go out of favor for years, leading to juicy initial yields. These big starting yields tempt investors into continually adding more. Additionally, during an inflated stock market, bargains are hard to find. These out of favor sectors look extra tempting for the DGI investor.

There are 11 sectors in the stock market, as defined by the Global Industry Classification Standard

(GICS). These sectors are a grouping of industries that fit under them. For instance, the financial sector consists of banks, insurance, mREITs, capital markets, consumer finance, financial services, and mortgage finance. The mREITs mentioned are a special class of REITS called mortgage real estate investment trusts. Most REITS fall into the real estate sector.

The complete list looks like this:

Communication services – 5 industries (diversified telecommunication services, entertainment, interactive media & services, media, and wireless telecommunication services)

Consumer discretionary – 11 industries (auto components, automobiles, distributors, diversified consumer services, hotels/restaurants/leisure, household durables, internet & direct marketing retail, leisure products, multiline retail, specialty retail, and textiles/apparel/luxury goods)

Consumer staples – 6 industries (beverages, food & staples retail, food products, household products, personal products, and tobacco)

Energy – 2 industries (energy equipment & services, and oil & gas/consumable fuels)

Financials – 7 industries (banks, capital markets, consumer finance, diversified financial services, insurance, mortgage REITs, and thrifts & mortgage finance)

Healthcare – 6 industries (biotechnology, healthcare equipment & supplies, healthcare providers & services, healthcare technology, life sciences tools & services, and pharmaceuticals)

Industrials – 14 industries (aerospace & defense, air freight & logistics, airlines, building products, commercial services & supplies, construction & engineering, electrical equipment, industrial conglomerates, machinery, marine, professional services, road & rail, trading companies & distributers, and transportation infrastructure)

Information technology – 6 industries (communications equipment, electronic equipment/instruments/components, IT services, semiconductors & semiconductor equipment, software, technology hardware/storage/peripherals)

Materials – 5 industries (chemicals, construction materials, containers & packaging, metals & mining, and paper& forest products)

Real estate – 2 industries (equity real estate, real estate management & development)

Utilities – 5 industries (electric utilities, gas utilities, independent power producers, multi-utilities, and water utilities)

While a DGI investor needs to understand these sectors, an individual investor may choose to categorize sectors differently based on their levels of risk and concerns. For instance, many DGI investors consider REITs a sector by itself for portfolio purposes. This classification can be reasonable for portfolio design purposes, as a bank's risks are different from an insurance company or REIT.

Most DGI investors will have rules regarding how much money to invest in each sector. These rules help to both spread risk out and to meet the goals of the portfolio.

It's unrealistic for a DGI portfolio to spread funds evenly across all the sectors and industries. Not all industries have suitable DGI companies. Instead, capping a sector at a certain percentage is better. A reasonable number is 15 to 20% of total income.

Diversifying across Positions

There was a time when it was difficult to get up to the date information on stocks, and the news was always a few days behind. Researching a company required digging thru financials and doing a lot of hand calculations. Only a few gate-keepers had access to all the information. Because of this, people to this day believe investing is hard.

Professional investment managers still insist that managing more than a few positions is too much work for most people. Given today's speed of information, this is nonsense — doubly nonsense for the DGI investor.

Today every investor has all the information they could ever need at the tip of their fingertips. There is no need to dig through annual reports to run calculations or have specialized computer programs to have up to the minute stock prices.

An investor trying to grow the overall portfolio balance may have more work to do to stay on top of the market. But a DGI investor begins with reliable companies and intends to hold them for a very long time. For this reason, there is no need for a DGI investor to watch prices closely, pour over annual reports, or read every news article.

At the very most, a DGI investor can keep a portfolio list in any one of a hundred different apps and scan for any large percentage changes in a position. They are looking for a large difference as compared to the market as a whole. The investor can then scan the news for anything of significance that might change a company's story. Which, to be frank, is quite rare.

In today's world, an investor should only limit the number of positions by their comfort level. It probably takes 20 or fewer stocks to achieve a satisfactory level of diversification. Indeed, an investor with the time and inclination can easily manage a portfolio with triple that number of positions.

"Everyone has the power to follow the stock market. If you made it through fifth grade math, you can do it." – Peter Lynch

Bucket Based Approach to DGI Portfolio Design

dividend freeze – A dividend freeze occurs when a company that typically increases its dividend on a regular schedule, fails to increase. Whereas a dividend cut is a reduction in the dividend, a freeze is keeping it the same.

spin-off – A spin-off occurs when a company breaks into two or more pieces creating new companies.

A common alternative to developing portfolios for a DGI investor is to take a bucket based approach. A bucket approach is different than using sectors. With this approach, the investor matches the portfolio's goals by lumping stocks into buckets. Each bucket contains stocks that add a distinct quality to the portfolio. Using buckets is more about managing future income sources than present-day risk. Whereas focusing on sectors is more about managing risk. Using both methods together is common to some degree.

This approach is generally more fluid than using hard rules for picking stocks. For example, an investor using this approach might be targeting initial yields of 3% and dividend growth of 10%. Sometimes there are attractive stocks that won't make the cut. Instead of achieving this thru purchasing only stocks that fit this criterion, the investor may have buckets that blend to meet this goal.

In this example, the investor may have a high yield bucket and a high growth bucket.

Let's say an investor has $2000 to invest in a new stock, but they can't find a bargain that fits the 3%/10% target they have established.

Instead, they find a bargain stock with a starting yield of 7%, but it only has a 5-year dividend growth rate of 2%. Additionally, there is another company they identify as a good buy, but it only has a starting yield of 2% but has a 5-year dividend growth rate of nearly 20%.

In this case, $500 invested in the high yield stock and $1500 in the lower-yielding one gives the desired result. Combining the two provides a starting yield of 3.3% and a 5-year dividend growth rate of 10.3%.

Interestingly enough, if the dividend growth rates remain constant, the growth rate will accelerate over time.

The calculation for this is as follows:

*Dividend from Stock ABC = $1500 * 2% = $30*
*Dividend from Stock XYZ = $500 * 7% = $35*
Total Dividend from $2000 purchase = $65
Total dividend yield = $105 / $2000 = 0.0325
or 3.25%

Expected 1 year dividend increase from
*ABC = $30 (current div) * 20% (5-year growth rate) = $6*
Expected 1 year dividend increase from
*XYZ = $35 * 2% = $0.7*
Total Expected increase = $6.70
Expected 1-year dividend growth = $6.7 / $65
(initial total dividend) = 0.103 or 10.3%

An investor could continue to purchase stocks in this manner to maintain targets. However, over time, the portfolio begins to become unwieldy. It is easy to lose track of the overall goal. There are just too many random positions. Buckets help solve this problem.

Just like when using a sector allocation, there are two ways to use buckets. These are with dividend income or by the portion of new investments. Either one is an excellent way to manage the dividend stream. An investor should never use buckets to allocate the portfolio's present-day value or rebalancing as it is known. Buckets should stay income focused.

Rebalancing is recommended by financial advisors with growth style portfolios to maintain the correct risk balance for the investor. Because a DGI investor focuses on income, this type of rebalancing is inappropriate for achieving the desired goals.

Typical buckets could include the following:

- High yield / No dividend growth
- High dividend growth
- Core dividend growth
- non-dividend stocks
- ETF's

High Yield Bucket

Just like the bucket name implies, these are high yielding stocks. They may or may not be dividend growth stocks. Companies in this bucket will likely carry a higher risk of the dividend being cut or frozen than other buckets. Generally, but not always, stocks with higher yields do so for a reason. Usually, this reason is that the consensus among investors is that the business is at risk. Two types of stocks fit into this bucket, slow dividend growth stocks and high dividend stocks that don't increase regularly.

Dividend growth stocks in this bucket usually have very low growth rates. Two percent would be common. Typical yields of a dividend growth stock in this bucket might be 5% or better, depending on how out of favor the industry is at the time. It's not uncommon for dividend champions to reach yields of greater than 7% in an out of favor industry. These typically include companies from the following sectors, but at times can consist of others: telecom, oil & gas, utilities, and tobacco.

An investor in high yield stocks that are not dividend growth stocks should require a higher starting yield to make up for the added risk of a dividend freeze or cut. Generally, these will be above 10%, and it should at least be significantly better than a high yielding dividend champion. An investor should set the bar high to take on the risk of a non-dividend achiever.

When to use this bucket:

There are two main reasons an investor will use this bucket. The first is because they plan to spend the income now. Think of a retiree who needs the income. The second is an investor who wants to increase the overall dividends collected to reinvest in faster dividend growth stocks. This second reason is particularly appealing early in a DGI investing career as it is motivating to see the overall income increase.

Risks and Concerns:

The high yield bucket can be a trap for many investors. It is tempting to want to see the portfolio's overall income grow at a faster rate. When an investor adds new funds to the high yield bucket, it can create an illusion that the dividend income is increasing rapidly. This growth is not high quality. As soon as new investment in the bucket stops, the income is at risk. Dividend growth from this bucket will grind to a halt, or even worse, begin to diminish.

The stocks falling in this bucket will be among the highest risk. During a market downturn, they will be highly punished both in price and the potential for dividend cuts. Even though a DGI investor shouldn't be concerned with the overall portfolio value, very few are immune to the psychology of losses.

Typical Bucket Size:

Because the two types of investors who mostly use this bucket will fall have very different goals, there is a wide range of appropriate investment into the high yield bucket.

A retiree or near retiree who is concerned about the total amount of income and less about growing the dividend income in the future will have a much bigger bucket allocation. Typically, this could be 50-70 percent of the total portfolio income produced. A higher range is more manageable when the bucket is primarily made up of dividend achievers, as the risk is lower.

A younger investor will want a much smaller high yield bucket. A smaller allocation allows the dividends to grow organically with high-quality stocks in other buckets. Typical ranges might be 0 – 20% of new capital invested in this bucket. With time, a younger investor may elect to phase out new investments.

The amount invested into this bucket will create a disproportionate amount of income due to the higher yields. When a portfolio is young, the investor will reinvest dividends into higher-quality companies that fall into other buckets. At some point, it makes sense for most investors to stop putting new money into this bucket altogether, at least until they are ready to start spending distributions. By not putting any further funds into this bucket, the investor will allow the dividend stream to maintain faster organic growth rates. Minimizing contributions into this bucket has a side effect of growing the overall portfolio value.

As an investor approaches retirement, they can always re-allocate into higher-yielding stocks if the additional income is needed or desired. Ideally, though, this bucket should be minimized as much as possible. The high yield bucket carries more risk and requires more time to manage.

High Dividend Growth Bucket

The high dividend growth bucket consists of companies with very high dividend growth and the potential to maintain this growth for an extended time. Usually, these companies will also have very low initial yields, in the 0.5% to 1.5% percent range. However, all stocks go on sale sometimes. At such times it may be possible to purchase at a much higher initial yield.

Usually, these stocks will be in younger industries, like software, fin-tech, or bio-tech. For this reason, most will not be on a dividend achiever list or will have relatively few years of dividend growth. These stocks will come with unique risks and potential that other buckets will not have.

Some companies that will fall into this bucket are large established companies that are still growing relatively fast. Most of these companies will generate enormous amounts of cash and just recently started a dividend program. Apple and Microsoft, in the mid-2010s, would be two examples of these types of companies. Because of the large cash flows, there is potential to increase the dividend rapidly for many years.

When to use this bucket:

Many risks exist in this bucket, but the potential is huge too. These companies have the potential to fuel future dividend growth for many years.

Additionally, these stocks could see massive capital growth over time.

Even though a DGI investor doesn't focus on overall portfolio value, that doesn't mean they don't like it. These stocks will have an inflated price to the dividend they produce. In the future, an investor can swap for higher-yielding stocks if the income is needed.

Younger investors, especially, should have a portion of the portfolio allocated into the high growth bucket.

Risks and Concerns:

The single biggest risk with stocks that fall into the high growth bucket is simply that the companies will tend to be younger in terms of years of dividend growth. Most of them will have relatively short dividend growth streaks. Less than ten years would be typical. As was discussed in the Dividend Achiever chapter, the longer a dividend growth streak, the more likely it will continue.

Often the companies falling into this bucket will be in faster moving industries. There exists a real possibility for new technology to come along and challenge the status quo. A company in these industries that doesn't continue to innovate may quickly lose any competitive advantage. Events like this could cause it to slow the dividend growth or eliminate the dividend.

Another consideration is the low starting yield. Psychologically, this is not easy to swallow when the overall goal is to create an income stream. Of course, with the rapid expected dividend growth rate, it should grow quickly. However, not many companies have sustained a 20% growth rate over many years.

Typical Bucket Size:

The nature of the "high dividend growth" bucket makes it a slightly more risky bucket, at least in terms of future dividends. Because of this, it will most of the time be a relatively low percentage of new capital invested. Typically this will range from 0 – 25%. Older and more conservative investors will be on the lower end and younger investors towards the higher end.

The vast majority of investors will keep this bucket under 10%. The small percentage is due to the low starting yields and short dividend growth histories. Accepting a 0.5% starting yield is difficult for nearly all investors in a world of instant gratification.

Core Dividend Growth Bucket

The "Core" bucket is the backbone of a DGI investor's portfolio. This bucket will consist of the strongest dividend achievers, typically with dividend growth streaks of at least 15 years. Typically, stocks in this bucket will have initial yields in the 2-4% range and 5-10% dividend growth rates.

Consider these the sleep-well-at-night stocks, or SWANs. These are the companies an investor plans to hold forever. An investor should focus most of their energy on stocks in this bucket as they make up the heart of the portfolio.

While no company is risk free, the companies in this bucket should have no glaring issues. As of 2020, a prime example of a core company would be Johnson & Johnson. This company has the highest possible debt rating (better than the US government!), grown the dividend annually for over 58 years, has a starting yield of around 3%, and a dividend growth rate of over 6%. And yet, Johnson & Johnson still has risks.

Every recall at Johnson & Johnson becomes doom and gloom for the company in our sensationalized news media. Yet the company does just fine. The news stories are just noise. However, real risks exist from competitors, health care reform, or any number of unforeseen situations.

The critical thing to notice is none of these are pressing and evident at the moment. An investor should monitor all core stocks, and the story evaluated. Just don't overthink it. These are SWAN companies.

Non-Dividend Bucket

This book is a guide to dividend growth investing. So, how do non-dividend stocks fit? For many DGI investors, they don't. However, some DGI investors may want to consider some non-dividend companies for their portfolio.

When to use this bucket:

Consider this a speculative bucket. This bucket is a place for investors who want to go for that "home run" stock that growth investors are always searching for, the one that goes up 100 times. The fact is DGI investing is boring. It is safe, consistent, and is a long-term strategy. Investors who have that need to play around a little can use this bucket as an outlet.

An investor may allocate part of their funds to a non-dividend bucket to capture future high dividend growth stocks. Many DGI investors believe that many of the non-dividend paying, mega-cap stocks that generate enormous cash flows will, at some point, begin paying a dividend and grow it quickly.

Risks and concerns:

There are obvious risks of investing in any non-dividend paying stocks. These risks are particularly real for a DGI investor. There is no guarantee the stocks will ever pay a dividend. But more importantly, there is a missed opportunity cost. By not investing in a stable dividend growth company, the investor is losing out on future income.

The other very real concern is similar to what can happen with a "high yield" bucket. With high yield stocks, an investor risks becoming addicted to seeing income grow quickly by taking on added risk. The investor loses sight of the goal of the portfolio. With non-dividend growth stocks, the cause is different, yet the result will be the same.

FOMO, fear of missing out is real. During the internet bubble of the late 1990s, anything associated with the internet or technology was going one direction, straight up. The vast majority of these companies had no profits and no clear path to do so. Everybody said it didn't matter; these were the companies of the future.

Anyone investing in dividend growth stocks during this bubble was missing out. A DGI investor with a non-dividend growth bucket watched as the value of this bucket grew and grew. How tempting was it to convert more and more of the portfolio into non-dividend growth stocks? When the bottom fell out of the market at the end of 1999, many of these investors gave up investing altogether, and most of the high-flying companies no longer exist. Microsoft, one of the few profitable bubble companies, took over 16 years to reach the same price it achieved in 1999.

At some point, a DGI investor who chases non-dividend stocks is no longer a DGI investor. They are a growth investor. Just as a DGI investor can get trapped into the high-yield bucket and become a high-yield investor, the same thing can happen with growth. Having a solid strategy and sticking to it is the key to being a successful investor, regardless of the investing style. Individuals who are continually shifting the portfolio strategy will have poor results over the long run.

Discipline is the key to dividend growth investing.

Typical allocation:

For all DGI investors, there is no need to use this bucket. Investors nearing retirement and plan to live off the income especially do not need this bucket. Although, some investors may want to incorporate non-dividend paying stocks into their portfolio for the above reasons.

The key is that an investor takes a disciplined approach with this bucket and keeps the allocation small. Generally, this should be less than 10% of the new capital put into the portfolio. However, some very young investors may consider going as high as 20%.

Bucket summary

One of the crucial things to remember about bucket allocation is that it can evolve. As the income stream grows in a portfolio, an investor may want to focus more on the core and high-growth buckets to foster future organic growth. Conversely, as an investor approaches retirement, they may begin allocating more funds into high-yield as organic growth might no longer be the primary goal.

There is no right number of buckets. Each individual needs to look at their personal goals and income needs. For instance, an older investor who is nearing retirement and plans to use the income immediately may focus more on the "high yield" bucket and may not include a "Non-dividend" bucket altogether.

A very young investor who has no plans to spend the income for many decades should focus on high dividend growth and core dividend growth. This investor may stay away from high yield altogether. It would also be appropriate for a younger investor to have a small bucket of non-dividend high growth stocks.

Investors who are afraid of missing out on the next monster growth stock may also want to have a small bucket of non-dividend companies. This bucket, in particular, should be monitored closely. It is easy to fall into the allure of the growth investing mindset.

Perhaps the single biggest mistake that DGI investors make is falling into the yield trap. That is chasing the high-yield bucket. Many investors have had their portfolios devasted by an economic downturn leading to multiple dividend cuts. In contrast, a disciplined DGI investor will continue to grow the income stream thru these downturns.

Author's Note

When I first started with DGI investing, I didn't use a defined bucket strategy. After I began analyzing my portfolio, I realized that the stocks fit into buckets nicely. Since then, I have found that many other DGI investors use this approach as well.

Early on, I didn't use a strict percentage per bucket. My purchases were pretty "loose," buying whatever I thought was a good bargain. However, I began to fall into the yield trap. My justification was that I would use the dividends collected to buy stocks growing the dividend faster. I still believe there is nothing wrong with this approach if disciplined and high-quality companies are purchased. Unfortunately, I made two big mistakes.

The first mistake I made was putting too much into this bucket. By over-allocating high-yield, I created a drag on the organic growth of dividends within my portfolio. In other words, to keep the dividend stream growing at a respectable clip, I had to keep buying more high yielding stocks. Unfortunately, with higher yields comes lower quality and slower dividend growth. Today I have rectified this, but I endured dividend cuts along the way.

The second mistake I made was in sector diversification. Many high yielding stocks tend to be in the same sectors. My portfolio became heavy in a couple of industries, particularly in energy, by over-buying high yielding stocks.

When oil crashed at the end of 2015, my energy companies' exposure was 25% of my dividends collected. This crash led to the worst year of dividend growth in my portfolio ever, with only a 6% increase in income for 2016.

Today, I use a combination of bucket allocation, income from each bucket, and sector diversification to drive new investments. Although I believe the high yield bucket is the most dangerous for a DGI investor, I still use it in exceptional situations. However, for the most part, my income stream is large enough that I don't need a "boost" from high dividend stocks. Instead, I focus primarily on the core bucket while keeping my eye out for bargains in the high dividend growth bucket.

While it is acceptable to use either dividends collected or new purchases as the percentages for each bucket, I use a hybrid approach. For most buckets, I use a percentage of new capital allocated. However, on the high-yield bucket, I also use a maximum percentage of income collected. I look at sectors differently.

When considering sectors, I look strictly at the income produced. The goal is to have no sector producing more than 15% of my total income. Additionally, I consider the individual stocks in each sector. For instance, the finance sector consists of many industries. If 15% of my income is from the finance sector, and it all comes from banks, this puts me at risk. If I divide the same 15% amongst banks, credit card issuers, and insurance companies, I am much more comfortable.

To be clear, I wouldn't let a single industry grow to 15% of my income. I don't set rules around this, but I do pay attention to it.

I do have other rules I incorporate into my portfolio as well. However, I treat everything as guidelines, not hard fast rules. This method works for me; other investors may want to keep their rules set in stone.

Below are my complete portfolio guidelines:

Bucket	New investment Allocation (%)	Maximum Income (% of total)
Core	82%+	Unlimited
High Yield	Less than 3%	Less than 15%
High Growth	10%	Unlimited
Non - Dividend	Less than 5%	N/A

1. No sector should be more than 15% of total income.
2. No individual stock should be more than 5% of total income.
3. No more than two companies owned per industry
4. All core companies purchased should be on a Dividend Achiever list, and the vast majority (85%) having at least a 15-year dividend growth history
5. For the core bucket, stocks should be targeted that have a 3%+ starting yield and a 7%+ 5-year dividend growth rate
6. No purchasing of mining companies, energy companies, or foreign companies (Explained in the miscellaneous chapter)

These have evolved over time. I focus much more on dividend growth rate and dividend safety today than I did in the past. Also, the non-dividend investments I make are only in a tax-deferred account. These investments are all companies that I believe will begin paying a dividend in the future.

As I said, these are my guidelines. Sometimes I have sectors that exceed the 15% rule, usually due to faster-growing dividends. When this happens, I just quit making new purchases in that sector. Additionally, it can be very tough to find companies yielding 3%, a 7% dividend growth rate, and at least 15 years of dividend growth. I am more lenient on the starting yield but balance this with either higher dividend growth or more years of dividend growth.

I recommend that everyone make their own set of guidelines. Investors should tailor to each's particular needs and goals. My goal is to have a portfolio that grows at 7% annually without reinvesting dividends and 10% annually when reinvesting dividends.

I effectively double my income every seven years pre-retirement and every ten years post-retirement by achieving this goal. This growth is assuming I add no additional capital to the portfolio.

"We don't have to be smarter than the rest, we have to be more disciplined than the rest." – Warren Buffett

When to Sell

A DGI investor purchases a stock with the intent to hold it forever. An investor should personally research a company, understand the story, and expect the company to be around for a long, long time. Selling a company like this should not be taken lightly.

Many DGI investors will have specific rules regarding selling. A common practice is to sell when a dividend is cut or frozen. Another is to sell when a company becomes wildly overvalued. Knowing when to sell is much harder than buying at a bargain price.

Probably the easiest "rule" to comprehend is selling a stock when it is wildly overvalued. Using this rule is also extremely difficult to do in practice. Examining this rule is why buying at a good price is much easier than selling at the right time.

When buying a stock, we are trying to purchase at a price that is better than average. Accomplishing this might be as simple as buying when the company pays better than the historical average dividend.

The investor is not trying to get the very best initial yield. After all, the investor can always purchase more if the price falls and the yield increases. The goal in this case, is to not overpay. The goal isn't to get the very best deal.

However, when selling a stock, a different set of reactions is at work. We wouldn't sell just because a stock isn't a good bargain for purchase. After all, historical averages are just that, averages. Half the time, something is above average; half is below. No matter how we define "wildly" overvalued, there is another challenge with selling.

A particular stock can stay overvalued for years. It's easy to say, "This is a great company, but it's way overvalued. I will sell it today and rebuy it when it's a bargain."

Unfortunately, this may or may not be the case. The company may continue to increase in price for years. Yes, it will almost certainly fall back to a bargain valuation, but this could be at a higher price than the investor sold it. Selling is the opposite of buying. While you can always buy more, there is no selling more.

Here is a better way to consider a stock that has become overvalued. Begin by asking a series of questions:

Why has the company become overvalued?

Does this reason affect the story?

Do I believe in the new story?

Is there an alternative to invest in that has a better story and metrics (initial yield, dividend growth, years of growth, or value)?

Will I regret not owning this stock ten years from now?

Answering these questions will help guide a decision on whether selling an overvalued stock is appropriate. The important thing to keep in mind is that great dividend growth companies will continue to grow the dividend over time. Dividend growth happens regardless of the current valuation.

The second common reason for selling a position is due to a dividend cut or freeze. Many DGI investors use this as a hard rule, with no exceptions. There is nothing wrong with having a hard rule like this. It makes investing much simpler. However, other investors may find it useful to dig a bit deeper.

There are many reasons a company might cut or freeze a dividend. Generally, cuts are much more indicative of a problem and should be a red flag for DGI investors. A dividend freeze requires more information upon which to act.

In either situation, an investor needs to look at the story. Consider the story at the time of purchase and how new information affects it.

A dividend cut usually occurs when a company sees something on the horizon that prevents it from prioritizing the dividend. Most often, this is due to a deteriorating financial outlook with no end in sight. Increased competition, failure to innovate, shrinking profit margins, or even the product not appealing to people anymore are all things that could dim a company's outlook. All of these lead to reduced profits, and when a company doesn't remedy them, it will lead to dividend cuts.

A second primary reason a company will cut the dividend is when it sees a need to retain the cash to grow the business. Most often, this will happen with companies with relatively short dividend growth histories. While these companies may still be stable, they will not be suitable for a DGI investor. This potential is yet another reason why investors should focus on companies with long dividend growth histories.

There is a type of dividend cut that is usually acceptable. In fact, it is typically a sign of a healthy company and good management. These are not even actual dividend cuts but can appear so when looking back at a company's past dividend history. These occur when a company spins off part of a company. These are called **spin-offs**. A company doing a spin-off creates two new companies. Although, one company will usually retain the old name.

It's essential to recognize that neither company will be the same as the old company when it splits. An investor should research each of these companies independently and separate stories created.

Reasons companies split include the following examples:

VF Corporation was a clothing company made up of many fast-growing brands but also included slower-growing legacy brands. In 2019, they split into two companies, one that could grow faster and one to maintain the slower growth brands.

Abbot labs was a medical device maker and drug manufacturing company. However, they had a colossal hit drug that was going to dominate the balance sheet. So, in 2013, the company split into two. The new Abbot labs would focus on medical devices and few other things while Abbvie would focus on drug research and manufacturing.

In 2012, Conoco Phillips was an integrated oil producer and refiner. The company decided to split the company to unlock shareholder value. They created two new companies. One maintained the ConocoPhillips name. Today, this company focuses on the exploration and production of oil and gas. The second company focuses on refining oil and gas products as well as the transportation of these products.

In all of these instances, none of the resulting companies was the same as the original company. Each new company has its own story and its own set of risks. Generally, when this occurs, the combined companies will have an equal or greater dividend than the original. However, each will create its dividend growth history going forward.

Dividend freezes are a different beast altogether.

While the vast majority of dividend cuts are a bad sign, dividend freezes are more nuanced. It's vital with freezes to understand the reason the company is stating for the freeze. Then to determine how the reason affects your story for the company.

Dividend growth companies experience two main types of freezes. One is more concerning to a DGI investor than the other. Whereas a dividend cut occurs because a company knows there is a problem, dividend freezes are a way for a company to take a "wait and see" position.

The first type of dividend freeze usually occurs after an acquisition or significant shift in the business. In this case, the company saves cash by freezing the distribution. Then they use the money saved to pay down debt from the acquisition or fund the business shift. These types of freezes need to be evaluated but are generally a sign of good management. They are not a cause for alarm. Often these companies will begin raising the dividend again in the future.

Some investors will sell a company on this type of freeze. This method is easier than evaluating the freeze. Additionally, not all companies will begin raising the dividend again. Many large acquisitions fail, and not all shifts in business succeed.

The second type of dividend freeze often proceeds a dividend cut. These are more common in companies with a long dividend history. They occur when something is happening or is on the horizon that could significantly affect the bottom line. Essentially the company believes the event will be short-lived.

A typical example of this occurs in the materials production industries, particularly mining and oil and gas production. Commodity prices go up and down with supply and demand. However, demand has always gone up over time. These companies tend to assume they can "ride it out."

This type of dividend freeze is usually a bad sign. A "choppy" dividend history is a warning sign. "Choppy" is when the company has grown the dividend for periods and then cut it, only to start growing it again. Additionally, when a company with a very long dividend growth history suddenly freezes the dividend, an investor should be extra concerned. A company with a long dividend growth history has seen many economic cycles and continued to grow the dividend. A sudden freeze is unusual and a cause for alarm.

The question the investor needs to ask is, "What's different this time?"

Often dividend achievers will use a near dividend freeze. This near-freeze is when the company grows the dividend very slowly, usually by only a penny or so a year. On a percentage basis, these might only be 1 or 2% growth. These companies often covet the dividend achiever status and don't want to lose it with a freeze.

An investor should evaluate a near-freeze the same as a dividend freeze. However, when the company continues to raise the dividend, it is generally a sign of strength, no matter how small the raise. In this situation, an investor should give extra consideration to a company's dividend growth streak. A 30-year growth company will be much more likely to continue growing the dividend than a company with ten years.

Authors note:

When I buy dividend growth companies, I intend to own them forever. Over the last decade, I have averaged less than two sales per year, and not all of these were entire positions. Many of the sales were because the company was being acquired. I took the instant stock price jump rather than wait and see if it happened.

I always sell on a dividend cut to a dividend growth stock. Period. No questions asked. However, many of the stocks in my high yield bucket are not dividend growth stocks. These I may or not sell. I'll explain how I determine what to do with these in just a bit.

I never sell based on valuation alone. Instead, I use a third reason to sell stocks. Actually, it's more of a method to determine if I should sell a stock.

I begin with understanding the philosophy of my portfolio: "Increase my dividend income thru organic growth," and the goal of my portfolio "Double my income every ten years without reinvesting dividends or every seven years with reinvesting dividends." These guide my decision process.

When selling a stock, I consider a blend of stock quality, current dividend yield, and dividend growth rate. Consider it an opportunity cost approach. At any given time, I know which stocks I consider the lowest quality in my portfolio.

Quality is subjective on my part. Generally, the stocks in the high yield bucket will be of lower quality than the core bucket. I base quality on how well I like the story, years of dividend growth, and dividend growth rate.

Then it's just a matter of comparing what is available in the stock market at any time. I begin by looking at my high yield bucket. Any non-dividend growing stocks are almost certainly the lowest quality. These are the first stocks I look to trade.

I will compare the current yield and compare that to the highest paying dividend growth stocks. If I can swap a non-dividend growth stock for a dividend growth stock with a similar yield, this immediately helps meet my goals. Additionally, any dividend achiever is probably higher quality than these stocks. Occasionally though, it is swapping a non-dividend growth stock for another with a much higher yield.

I will do the same thing with stocks in the core bucket. Only with this bucket, I use both yield and dividend growth. If I can take a lower quality stock and swap it for a higher quality one with a similar current yield but better growth rate, this helps meet my portfolio's goal.

When I am looking at the core bucket, I don't rank every stock. Instead, I determine the lowest three or five in terms of quality relative to the others. These are the ones I consider swapping out.

Swapping out a core stock isn't easy. These were all bought to hold forever. I consider what selling the stock will do to the overall portfolio in terms of sector balance. The other consideration is that even the best dividend growth stocks will go thru times of slow growth. If you study the dividend growth history of any company, it is evident that dividend growth is usually lumpy.

When I sell a core bucket holding, one of two things has happened most of the time. The first is a company has dramatically increased in price, and it has become a large percentage of the portfolio. While at the same time, it is in the lower tier of quality. I rarely sell the entire position in these situations but will trim it back to a comfortable holding percentage.

The second thing that causes me to consider selling is a loss of faith in its story. Occasionally the story changes to the point I no longer believe the company will sustain its dividend. In this case, I always look to swap as soon as possible. The issue is more often that I question the company's ability to maintain a suitable dividend growth rate. If an attractive enough alternative exists, I might sell the entire position, but usually, I will keep a part of it as a hedge in case I am wrong.

There is one other situation where I nearly always sell a stock. It wasn't mentioned above because it is not related to dividend growth investing in particular. This situation is when a company is going to be acquired. When a company announces that it's being bought, the stock will jump in price. It will likely not make it to the planned buyout price, but it will be within a few cents. I usually sell before the buyout.

There are a few reasons I sell in this situation. The primary one being, acquisitions sometimes fall apart. They have to get shareholder approval, regulatory approval, and any number of problems could arise that cancel the sale. Instead, I take my money upfront. Another reason is that often these take time. It's not uncommon for the acquired company to halt its dividend during the process.

The way I handle selling stocks has been an evolution over many years. Everyone should make considerations based on their own portfolio goals.

I would just assume never to sell a company, but there are times it is necessary. I believe there would be nothing wrong with only having one rule on selling a stock: Only sell on a dividend cut.

"One of the funny things about the stock market is that every time one person buys, another sells, and both think they are astute." – William Feather

ETFs in Dividend Growth Investing

So far, we have only discussed individual stocks. However, not every DGI investor enjoys researching companies and waiting for a bargain price. Many investors will use ETFs instead. A DGI investor can build an entire portfolio out of ETFs, or they can be used as a separate "bucket" to enhance a portfolio.

First, what is an ETF? ETF stands for exchange-traded fund. They are a basket of stocks that trade on an exchange just like a stock. They are similar to mutual funds but are usually more cost-effective and easy to trade.

There is an ETF for nearly anything imaginable. For the DGI investor, relevant ones include high yield, dividend growth, dividend aristocrats, dividend kings, stable income, and more. Many of these specialize in small-cap, foreign stocks, large-cap, and nearly anything imaginable. However, the more specialized the ETF, the more risk exists, and generally, the higher the fees.

With all this diversification available, the question becomes, "Why wouldn't everyone just build a portfolio out of ETF's?" There is absolutely nothing wrong with doing just that. Building a portfolio entirely out of ETFs has many advantages, but it does have some drawbacks.

Many investors want to buy positions when the stock is a clear bargain. When an ETF is purchased, you are buying every company in the basket. At any given time, the ETF includes overpriced companies. A lot of investors would rather choose the timing of purchasing these stocks.

Additionally, ETFs have management fees. The management fees on ETFs tend to be very small when compared to mutual funds. Still, as we get into more specialized ETFs, the costs tend to go up. Additionally, no matter how small the fees, they always reduce an investor's return. Many investors would rather not pay fees.

Understanding these downsides in ETFs are important to understand. There are many reasons to use ETFs in a portfolio as well. Each investor should weigh their circumstance and decide accordingly.

As mentioned, some investors don't like researching and picking individual stocks. That is not the only reason a DGI investor might use an ETF. They can be handy for a new investor to achieve diversification or enhance a particular bucket in an established portfolio. They are also useful for an investor who wants to transition from actively managing towards a more passive system.

ETFs can be beneficial to an investor who is just starting to build a dividend growth portfolio. It isn't easy to achieve a diversified portfolio and buy at discounted prices. It's challenging because different sectors come in and out of favor over time.

A patient investor who is comfortable being rather heavy in a few sectors early on will eventually achieve diversification. However, this could take years when only buying at bargain prices. An investor can always maintain diversification if they are willing to pay a premium on some sectors and industries.

Instead, a DGI investor who is just beginning to build a portfolio can focus primarily on ETFs. In this way, the investor has instant diversification. Diversification reduces risk. From this point, the investor can add individual stocks as bargains come up.

A good starting point with this method would be to use an 80% ETF bucket and 20% in individual stocks. Over time as the portfolio adds more individual positions, the stocks will begin to diversify. As the stocks diversify, the investor can reduce the percentage of new funds placed into the ETF bucket.

The other spot where ETF's can be particularly useful is as a replacement within an established portfolio. Usually, this occurs within the smaller percentage buckets, like high dividend, non-dividend, or high potential. However, an investor who wants to focus energy on high potential or non-dividend stocks could use an ETF to replace the "core" bucket.

Using an ETF in place of the "high dividend" or "high potential" buckets makes a lot of sense. Both these buckets can be harder to manage. These buckets tend to require more work because they are higher risk. There is simply more to watch. Higher risk leads to more maintenance, that is, time spent reviewing them. In contrast, high-quality stocks with long dividend growth histories require very little time and attention.

The non-dividend bucket can require a different approach. Some investors may want to place all this money into a large company. They are betting that the company will begin paying a dividend someday with the large cashflows. Examples are the famous FANG stocks, Facebook, Amazon, Netflix, and Google.

But often, investors like the non-dividend bucket to try for home runs. The best way to do this is to make many small bets. The reason for using many small bets is that the majority of these companies will fail, but some will hit it big. An ETF provides this diversification with little work.

There is no right or wrong way to use ETFs within a dividend growth portfolio. Some investors use them exclusively, and some use them as supplements for added diversification. Others don't use them at all.

Author's note:

I have never been a big fan of using ETFs in my portfolios. The thought of paying too much for a company always bothers me. However, as I grow older, ETFs are growing more appealing. While I do enjoy evaluating stocks, the draw of a set and forget portfolio is growing.

This appeal is especially true in the high potential area of my portfolio. At this point, I am so familiar with most companies with at least 25 years of dividend growth that I don't spend much time analyzing them—however, many of the high potential companies I am not.

I also know that current income will become more important than the income growth at some point. I have started using ETFs in my high-dividend bucket. Today, I make more use of high dividend ETFs instead of individual stocks. Spending a lot of time with these stocks is not enjoyable for me. And after all, do-it-yourself investing should be enjoyable!

> *"Index investing outperforms active management year after year." – Jim Rogers*

Odds and Ends

This chapter focuses on topics, questions, and misconceptions that often come up in dividend growth investing. Most of these are brief discussions that don't fall into anywhere else.

Should I DRIP dividends?

DRIP stands for a dividend reinvestment plan. Many companies offer this to investors to immediately use the dividend to buy more shares. Today many brokerages do the same and just call it automatic dividend reinvestment.

At one time, this method held great appeal. Transaction fees were high on buying stocks, and a DRIP was free. Today we have seen online brokerages go from very low fees to no fees at all. So, this reason no longer applies unless, for some reason, an investor chooses to use a brokerage that charges fees.

The other appeal for reinvesting dividends is that it forces the investor to buy more of a company. Some companies that grow fast always look expensive. So dividend reinvestment is a way to continue to add to the position. Of course, this is the same reason many investors choose not to use automatic reinvestment. They don't want to put money in overpriced companies automatically.

Many investors, probably most DGI investors, would rather have more control over the reinvestment of dividends. That is because they only want to buy shares at bargain prices.

Either is fine, and both methods have their arguments. Many investors will turn on automatic reinvestment for stocks that they believe are at fair prices and turn it off for overpriced companies. Of course, turning it on and off requires more work.

Foreign Stocks (Non-US)

Occasionally you will hear someone say that you need foreign stocks for diversity. Sometimes foreign companies seem novel and exciting. There is nothing wrong with using them in a DGI portfolio, but there are some drawbacks.

Foreign stocks do not add significant diversity to a DGI portfolio. Most of the companies in the DGI universe are multinational companies and will have sales worldwide. The worldwide sales by these companies creates foreign exposure. For many companies that are US based but have a large percentage of revenues from overseas, this can be a problem. Swings in exchange rates can, at times, have large impacts on the company's financials. Not that this is a massive problem for most companies. It does lead to one of the issues with foreign stocks in a DGI portfolio.

The key to a DGI portfolio is investing in stocks that consistently grow dividends. Foreign companies report earnings and pay dividends in their local currency. Because exchange rates are constantly changing, this creates uneven distributions for the US investor.

Probably the more significant issue for most DGI investors is foreign taxes. Many countries will take a foreign tax right off the top upon paying the dividend. Some of these are up to 30%! This tax immediately reduces the income received from the published yield.

For the most part, foreign taxes are recouped in tax credits or deductions when filing annual income taxes. Many investors don't want to deal with this added tax complexity. DGI investors interested in using foreign stocks in a portfolio should consult with an accountant to understand foreign taxes' full issues.

Aren't high dividend stocks risky?

It's easy to find articles warning of the risks of high dividend stocks. On message boards, you can often find newer investors shouting about how a high dividend is a sign the company is about to go bankrupt, and it needs to eliminate the distribution.

Imagine XYX company paid a $5 dividend and had a payout ratio of 50%. Last year the company was trading at $100 per share. This payout equates to a 5% dividend yield, $5/$100. This yield would generally be considered reasonable and is undoubtedly a safe payout ratio.

The next year a severe recession hits, and the stock market tanks. The crash leaves the price of XYZ at $50 per share. The company maintains sales and believes that next year revenue will grow. XYZ company leaves the dividend unchanged at $5 while still maintain a 50% payout ratio. The current dividend yield is 10% ($5/$50). Is XYZ company a risky investment?

A yield of 10% by many would be considered high risk. Is there anything in the above scenario that indicates the XYZ is likely to cut the dividend? Of course not! Instead, the company appears to be a bargain, and most DGI investors would be looking to snap up shares.

Of course, this is a simplified example to show the absurdity of making a blanket statement that high dividends are risky. In the real world, such examples are rarely clear cut. It's essential to weigh the company's dividend history, its story, and overall market and sector sentiment.

The fact remains that most high dividend stocks are risky, at least riskier than core dividend growth stocks. Many of them will have erratic dividend histories. However, occasionally a dividend achiever will become a high yield company. These achievers should be examined closely for inclusion in the high yield bucket of a portfolio.

Dealing with Spin-offs

A spin-off is when a company splits off part of the company into a new company. When a company "spins" a significant portion of itself, it will create two new companies. Neither new company will maintain the same business as the old company. Although usually in this situation, one of the companies will keep the old name.

When this occurs, it is usually positive for the stockholders. Some very conservative DGI investors will immediately sell the new company upon the spin-off and examine the old company. They look closely because the new company will have no established dividend history. However, in most instances, this has proven to be the wrong choice.

Spin-offs usually continue the original company's policy of distributing and raising dividends. However, an investor should evaluate both companies on their own merits. If the old company had great management, the new ones likely do as well, but the new story needs to be determined.

A good example of this was ConocoPhillips. In 2012, ConocoPhillips split into two new companies. Before this split, they were considered the best managed integrated oil producer. An integrated oil producer produces oil and gas, maintains a distribution system, and refines products. They split into ConocoPhillips, an oil and gas producer, and Phillips 66, which contained the distribution system and refinery. Even though one company retained the old name, it was a very different company going forward.

Integrated oil and gas companies have some control over the swings in oil and gas prices because they have other parts of the business that can make up profits when the prices of the commodity are down. In the future, it was apparent that the new ConocoPhillips would be unable to do this. And, when oil crashed in 2016, they cut the dividend sharply.

In this example, the dividend risk was apparent by examining the new companies' stories. Investors should note that the combined dividend of the two companies has continued to grow. Other examples of dividend champions that have spun off companies include the following: Altria into Kraft, Altria, and Phillip Morris; Abbot Labs into Abbot Labs and Abbvie; and VF Corporation into VF Corporation and Kontoor Brands.

All of these other examples have continued to pay and grow dividends, except for Kraft. However, time will tell with the VF Corporation spinoff as they split recently as of this writing.

Sometimes, a company will spin-off just a small piece of the company. Perhaps a division that doesn't quite fit into the core business. In these instances, it is possible the company attempted to sell the piece for cash and was unable to find a buyer. These spinoffs are usually relatively small, and most DGI investors will sell them as they rarely add to their portfolios.

The bottom line is that when a dividend champion spins off a company, an investor should evaluate each piece. Almost all the time, these companies will continue to pay and grow a dividend going forward. And sometimes, part of the company will have significant growth unlocked and be able to raise the dividend quickly.

There is an offer to acquire a company in your portfolio

From time to time, one company will offer to acquire one that you own. For the growth investor, this is an immediate boon, as the price will generally jump instantly. Unfortunately, for the dividend growth investor, this a problem. The DGI investor buys with the intent of holding for decades. Now the investor has decisions to make and work to do.

It is important to keep in mind that not all acquisitions end up going through. Usually, regulatory and shareholder hurdles exist. However, the companies involved are reasonably confident it will go forward before announcing.

The first thing to consider is the nature of the acquisition. If it's an all-cash deal, it should be a no brainer for the DGI investor. Sell the stock immediately. This decision is easy because there is a small chance the sale will not go through, and the stock price will fall back down. Additionally, acquisitions can take a while to occur, and it is not uncommon for a company to suspend the dividend during the final steps of being acquired.

Note that the investor will leave a few dollars on the table by selling immediately. An offer of $100 per share for a company will result in a stock price slightly below $100. This slight discount occurs because of the small chance the deal won't go ahead. However, by waiting, the investor loses the opportunity to redeploy the money elsewhere.

A more common acquisition is an all-stock or combination stock and cash acquisition. In the first, the investor receives shares in the acquiring company only and the latter a combination of shares and cash. In these types of acquisitions, the investor must investigate the acquiring company to see if it fits their portfolio. If it does, it may make sense to sit tight and let the deal happen.

Many investors will still elect to sell the stock before the acquisition. The price premium the acquiring company is paying will cause the stock to jump in price regardless of it being a stock or cash deal. When the investor sells, the gain is locked in. Then in the event the acquisition falls through, they can always rebuy at a lower price.

Your portfolio looks like an index

There is an interesting thing that happens over time with a DGI portfolio. Over time the portfolio will begin to resemble that of an index or ETF. This phenomenon occurs when an investor is staying diversified and only buying companies at bargains.

This begs the question…if the portfolio looks like an index, why not just buy an ETF?

Well, this goes back to the discussion in the ETF section. Many investors don't want to buy all the stocks in an ETF all the time. They only want to invest in the ones that are bargains. Additionally, an ETF may hold many companies that an investor has no desire to own. Other investors just enjoy selecting stocks and want the control that comes with individual positions.

How does your return compare to the S&P 500?

Investors often use the S&P 500 as a measuring stick. This measure is relevant if the goal is to beat the S&P 500. Let's repeat that: If your goal is to beat the S&P 500, then comparing returns to the S&P 500 makes sense. The question then becomes, "Is your goal to beat the S&P 500?"

For a DGI investor, this answer should be "No." DGI investors focus on growing dividend income, and a portfolio's total return has no bearing on income growth. The relevant questions for DGI investors revolve around income growth.

However, most DGI portfolios will approximate the returns of the S&P 500. Some years will likely be a little higher, some a little lower. But this is just a vanity metric. It has no bearing on the goal of the portfolio. Unless, of course, one of an individual's portfolio goals happens to be to beat the S&P 500.

A DGI investor should focus on growing the dividend income and leaving total returns to other investing styles.

The dividend is too small to make it worthwhile

One of the hardest things about getting started is that initial dividend collections are small. Small distribution checks can lead to a feeling that the dividend just isn't worth it. Small yields don't work for a high dividend investor, as they don't meet the investment goal. However, the DGI investor is more focused on the future dividend.

For example, a $1000 invested in a company with a starting yield of 3% will bring in $30 of income. This dividend doesn't sound like very much. But, if the dividend is growing at 10% annually, it will double approximately every seven years. After seven years, the distribution will be $60, 14 years $120, and 21 years $240! All from a $1000 investment. When the dividends collected are reinvested into more stock, this growth compounds even faster!

Dividend growth investing is a long game. Often investors will use motivations. These can be simple things like making enough dividend income to pay a utility bill or mortgage payment. Others think of dividends in terms of how many hours of work they replace. Anything that helps the investor see progress.

Growth stocks always beat other types of investing

There are times when growth stocks have significantly outperformed value stocks. There are periods when value stocks have significantly outperformed growth stocks. Just like sectors and industries come in and out of favor, so do value vs. growth, large-cap vs. small-cap, and other ways to segregate stocks.

Between 2009 and 2019, Amazon returned approximately 1,250%! $500 invested in Amazon at its IPO in 1997 would be worth $1 million at the end of 2020. Why wouldn't everyone want to invest in growth stocks?

The fact is the vast majority of investors who try to beat the market (in this case, the S&P 500 benchmark) will fail. For every Amazon, hundreds of companies fail to succeed, let alone become unstoppable forces.

Dividend growth investing is simple and takes away most of the headaches that come along with growth investing.

- In both the 1999 and 2008 market crashes, the S&P 500 dropped nearly 50% from its high. In both these cases, it took over six years for the market to regain its all-time high. Growth investors will say you can generate an income

stream by just selling stock. This theory is great until the market is down 50%.
- DGI investing is a relatively simple method of investing and does not take extensive watching of the market
- Markets go up, and markets go down, DGI investors keep collecting an ever-growing income stream.
- The dividend achievers offer a pre-built list of stocks to choose from instead of the infinite realm and research of growth stocks.
- Long term investing strategies like DGI discourage lots of trading. A portfolio is like a bar of soap. The more you handle it, the smaller it gets. Studies show that investors who trade often have the worst returns.

Analyst Ratings

There is an interesting fact about analysts. Nobody ever scores their accuracy. They can make all the predictions in the world about whether a stock is a buy or hold and target prices. But nobody is keeping score if they are right.

These ratings have no practical use for a DGI investor and can only hurt. None of them are looking at the long term. In contrast, a DGI investor should be looking 20 years out.

Now, while analyst ratings are useless to the DGI investor, Morningstar ratings are different. These are ratings of relative value and risk. Many DGI investors will use these as a metric in evaluating companies.

"If stock market experts were so expert, they would be buying stock, not selling advice." – Norman Ralph Augustine

Common Mistakes and Pitfalls

One of the best things about DGI investing is that it's tough to mess up. Stick to dividend achievers, diversify across sectors and industries, don't let a single position account for too much income, and invest for the long term. Pretty simple. There are a couple of traps an investor should watch for, however.

Don't chase yield!

The single most common mistake DGI investors make is focusing too much on the initial yield. Investors fall into this trap because they want to see the income grow faster. A 5% initial yield sounds better than a 2% starting yield. While higher dividend stocks have a place in most DGI portfolios, the investor needs to take caution not to let the initial yield become the portfolio driver.

Most of the time, but not all the time, a higher starting yield comes with trade-offs. The most obvious is adding risk. Stocks with higher yields are usually out of favor, possibly indicating a problem with the company. Additionally, frequently these companies will have a shorter dividend growth history. The fewer years a company has been increasing its dividend, the more risk exists.

Assuming the DGI investor completes due diligence and determines the risk is acceptable, a second likely issue occurs. This is in dividend growth. Often, companies that have long dividend growth histories and high yields will have very low growth rates. Investing heavily in companies like this will eventually affect the growth of an income stream.

Many DGI investors have fallen into the yield trap. If not caught in time, these investors often suffer multiple dividend cuts during economic downturns. Too much emphasis on yield and ignoring quality and dividend growth is the single biggest mistake a DGI investor can make.

Ignore the headlines!

Nearly every media source has one goal: To get an audience to tune in. The media focusses on attention-grabbing headlines and predictions. These have no place in a DGI investor's world.

Tune in to CNBC someday. An investor who follows the recommendations would continuously be turning over their portfolio. The talking heads have no idea about that investor or their goals. They need short term thinking to keep people watching. Talking about a company's future 20 years out is boring. Boring is not good for viewership.

Nearly any media source follows the same pattern. For every article praising a company, there are just as many predicting a company's doom.

An investor should carefully evaluate sources of information on individual stocks. Small blogs and podcasts are generally the best sources. Television, magazines, and large blogs need a large viewership to fund their business model and have the incentive to sensationalize to get the most eyeballs. Whereas smaller blogs and podcasts usually work with a much smaller but more focused audience. Still, with any source, an investor needs to evaluate carefully. Over time it will become apparent if the content matches the investor's particular goals and needs.

Most headline events have no significant impact on an investor with a long term view. Although, there are a few events that should be big red warning flags. These usually involve accounting scandals. Anytime accounting issues hit the news or a CFO (Chief Financial Officer) suddenly retires, it is time to reassess a position.

For the most part, sticking to high-quality dividend growth stocks means an investor can sleep well at night and ignore the pundits.

Avoid Portfolio Drift

Portfolio drift is an unconscious action. It occurs when an investor starts with one philosophy or goal, and it changes over time, but not on purpose. This shift is different than intentionally spelling out a change in bucket allocations within a portfolio.

One type of portfolio drift is focusing too much on yield, as discussed above. However, the same thing can occur with non-dividend paying stocks. It's easy to fall into this trap when the stock market reaches points of irrationality in valuations. FOMO is real! When it feels like everybody is making big gains in stocks with no actual earnings and no clear path to profits, it can be tempting to abandon DGI investing. This temptation is especially real for investors who haven't experienced a prolonged market downturn.

At times like these, it is doubly important to understand the portfolio goals. If an investor wants to adjust bucket contributions, it is vital to do so intentionally. It's very easy to plan on contributing funds to other buckets in the future and catch them back up. Once this is occurring, the investor has already abandoned their strategy.

"I love quotes… but in the end, knowledge has to be converted to action or it's worthless." – Tony Robbins

Definitions

buyback – When a company performs a buyback, it is buying back shares of its own company. This is the opposite of dilution and increases the EPS as fewer shares exist.

cost basis – The cost basis is the original purchase price of a stock.

dilution – Stock dilution is when a company issues more shares thereby reducing the percentage of the company owned by prior shareholders. This in turn reduces the EPS of the company as the earnings are now divided by more shares.

dividend cut – A dividend cut is a reduction in the dividend from the previous payout. For dividend growth investors this is usually measured on an annual basis.

dividend freeze – A dividend freeze occurs when a company that typically increases its dividend on a regular schedule, fails to increase. Whereas a dividend cut is a reduction in the dividend, a freeze is keeping it the same.

dividend growth rate – The dividend growth rate is the annualized rate, expressed as a percentage, that a dividend has grown over a set amount of time. Usually this is expressed as a 1-year, 5-year, or 10-year growth rate.

dividend growth stock – A dividend growth stock is a company that steadily increases dividends over time.

dividend safety – Dividend safety refers to how likely is a dividend likely to be cut or reduced. A safe dividend is unlikely to be cut.

dividend yield – The dividend yield is a ratio of the amount of money a company pays shareholders for owning a share of stock divided by its current stock price. This is expressed as a percentage and usually on an annual basis.

economic cycle – The economic cycle is the fluctuation of the economy between periods of growth and contraction.

earnings per share (EPS) – The EPS is a financial calculation that divides the total earnings of a company divided by the total number of shares. This results in the earnings attributed to each individual share.

ETF – An exchange traded fund (ETF) is a basket of stocks traded as a single unit on an exchange.

initial yield – The initial yield is the dividend yield an investor expects to receive at the time a stock is purchased.

Market capitalization – Commonly referred to as market cap, the market capatilization of a company is its total number of shares times the current share price. Companies are commonly referred to as large-cap, small-cap, mid-cap, and micro-cap.

>**large cap** – A large cap stock is a company with market capitalization above $10B.

>**small cap** – A small cap stock is a company with a market capitalization of between $300M and $2B.

MLP – A master limited partnership (MLP) is a business venture that exists as a publicly traded limited partnership. For this reason, it has some of the tax benefits of a partnership but is easy to trade like a public stock.

payout ratio – The dividend payout ratio is the amount of dividends paid to investors as a percentage of earnings. Sometimes this is expressed as a percentage of cash flow.

PE Ratio – A PE ratio, is short for price-to-earnings ratio of a stock. It is calculated by dividing a company's stock price by its earnings-per-share.

portfolio – A portfolio is a collection of stocks.

REIT – A real estate investment trust (REIT) is a company that owns, operates, or finances income producing properties. A special class of REITs called mREITs focus on mortgages.

spin-off – A spin-off occurs when a company breaks into two or more pieces creating new companies.

"The best thing a human being can do is to help another human being know more." – Charlie Munger

Questions or Comments?

I'd love to hear your thoughts. Email me at jesse@incomegrowthinvesting.com

And if you took value from this book, please help spread the word by leaving a review at Amazon.com. Thank you for reading!

Sign up to receive free DGI resources!

Sign up at https://info.incomegrowthinvesting.com/free-resources to receive resources to help you on your DGI journey. In addition to a list of resources, you will receive exclusive content that I don't share anywhere else. Including a monthly newsletter full of insights into the current state of the market for DGI investors, my personal portfolio moves, as well as company recommendations and reviews.

Made in the USA
Las Vegas, NV
04 September 2023